# ESTATE PUBLICATIONS

G000252389

# LINCOLNSHIRE

## Street maps with index
## Administrative Districts
## Population Gazetteer
## Road Map with index
## Postcodes

Street plans prepared and published by ESTATE PUBLICATIONS, Bridewell House, TENTERDEN, KENT.
The Publishers acknowledge the co-operation of the local authorities
of towns represented in this atlas.

Ordnance Survey® This product includes mapping data licensed from Ordnance Survey®
with the permission of the Controller of Her Majesty's Stationery Office.

# COUNTY RED BOOK

# LINCOLNSHIRE

### contains street maps for each town centre

## SUPER & LOCAL RED BOOKS

### are street atlases with comprehensive local coverage

## GRIMSBY & CLEETHORPES

including: Great Coates, Holton le Clay, Humberston, Immingham, Laceby, Waltham, Yarborough etc.

## KINGSTON UPON HULL

including: Barton-upon-Humber, Beverley, Cottingham, Elloughton, Hedon, Hessle, Hornsea, Withernsea etc.

## LINCOLN

including: Bracebridge Heath, Cherry Willingham, Nettleham, North Hykeham, Skellingthorpe, Sudbrooke, Washingborough etc.

## PETERBOROUGH

including: Deeping St. James, Hampton, Market Deeping, Stamford, Whittlesey, Yaxley etc.

## SCUNTHORPE

including: Berkeley, Bottesford, Broughton, Crosby, Frodingham, Riddings, Westcliff, Yaddlethorpe etc.

# CONTENTS

COUNTY ADMINISTRATIVE DISTRICTS:                    pages 4-5

GAZETTEER INDEX TO ROAD MAP:                        pages 6-7
(with populations)

COUNTY ROAD MAP:                                    pages 8-11

## TOWN CENTRE STREET MAPS:

---

### LEGEND TO STREET MAPS

| One-Way Street | → | Post Office | ● |
|---|---|---|---|
| Pedestrianized | ▨ | Public Convenience | Ⓖ |
| Car Park | ℗ | Place of Worship | + |

**Scale of street plans: 4 Inches to 1 mile (unless otherwise stated on the map).**

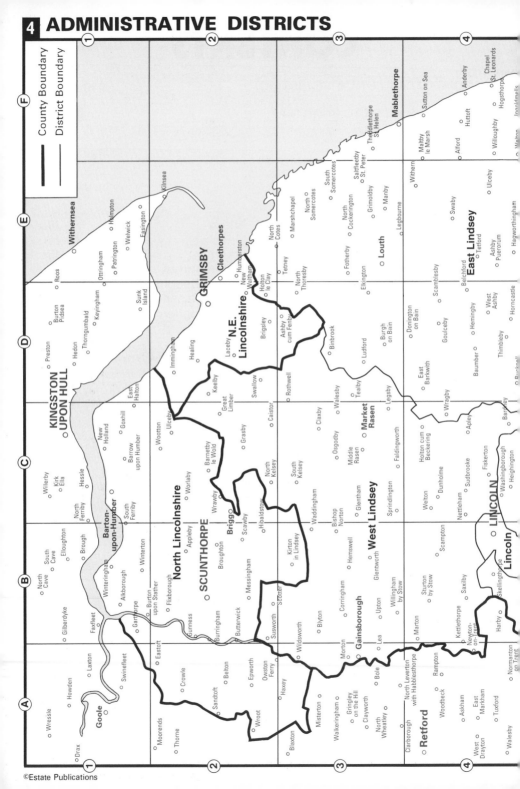

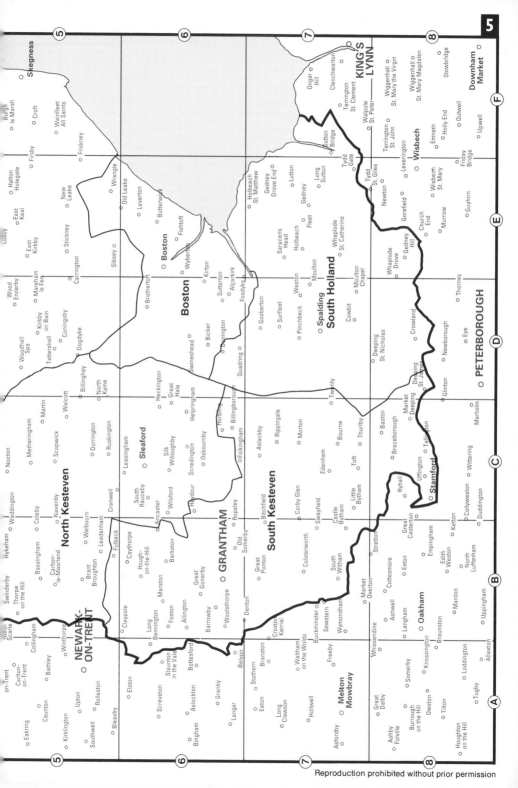

# GAZETTEER INDEX TO ROAD MAP
## with Populations

County of Lincolnshire population **896,446**
including the parts of Humberside that are now North and North East Lincolnshire

**LINCOLNSHIRE Districts:**

| District | Population |
|---|---|
| Boston | 53,226 |
| East Lindsey | 116,957 |
| Lincoln | 81,987 |
| N.E. Lincolnshire | 159,662 |
| North Kesteven | 79,942 |
| North Lincolnshire | 152,248 |
| South Holland | 67,261 |
| South Kesteven | 108,945 |
| West Lindsey | 76,218 |

Aby with Greenfield 210 — 9 G6
Addlethorpe 320 — 9 H6
Aisby — 8 B4
Aisby — 10 C3
Aisthorpe 82 — 8 C5
Alford 2,989 — 9 G6
Algarkirk 438 — *
Alkborough 454 — 8 B1
Allington 666 — 10 B3
Althorpe with Keadby 1,733 — 8 B3
Alvingham 23 — 9 F4
Amber Hill 303 — 11 E3
Amcotts 225 — 8 B2
Ancaster 1,134 — 10 C3
Anderby 311 — 9 H6
Anderby Creek — 9 H6
Anton's Gowt — 11 F2
Anwick 304 — 10 D3
Apley 74 — 8 D6
Appleby 606 — 8 C2
Asgarby — 11 F1
Asgarby & Howell 65 — 10 D3
Ashby 7,433 — 8 B3
Ashby cum Fenby 217 — 9 E3
Ashby de la Launde & Bloxholm 243 — 10 D2
Ashby with Scremby 136 — 11 G1
Aslackby & Laughton 243 — 10 D4
Asterby 98 — *
Aswarby & Swarby 129 — 10 D3
Aswardby 42 — 9 F6
Aubourn Haddington & Sth Hykeham 702 — 10 B1
Aunsby & Dembleby 132 — 10 D3
Authorpe 119 — 9 G5
Authorpe Row — 9 H6
Aylesby 128 — 9 E3
Bardney 1,724 — 8 D6
Barholm & Stowe 78 — 10 D6
Barkston 464 — 10 C3
Barlings 448 — *
Barnetby le Wold 1,444 — 8 D3
Barnoldby le Beck 223 — 9 E3
Barrow upon Humber 2,161 — 8 D2
Barrowby 2,084 — 10 B3
Barton upon Humber 9,422 — 8 C1
Bassingham 1,043 — 10 B1
Bassingthorpe Bitchfield 118 — 10 C4
Baston 689 — 10 D6
Baumber 220 — 9 E6
Beckingham 263 — 10 B2
Beelsby 115 — 9 E3
Beesby with Saleby 235 — 9 G5
Belchford 236 — 9 F6
Belleau 28 — 9 G6
Beltoft — 8 A3
Belton 2,549 — 8 A3
Belton & Manthorpe 185 — 10 C3
Benington 538 — 11 G3
Benniworth 195 — 9 E5
Bicker 679 — 11 E3
Bigby 248 — 9 E3
Billingborough 917 — 10 D4
Billinghay 1,707 — 10 D2
Bilsby 385 — 9 G6
Binbrook 800 — 9 E4

Birchwood — 8 C6
Birkholme — 10 C5
Bishop Norton 265 — 8 C4
Bitchfield & Bassingthorpe 118 — 10 C4
Blankney 262 — 10 D1
Bloxholm & Ashby de la Launde 243 — 10 D2
Blyborough 91 — 8 C4
Blyton 976 — 8 B4
Bolingbroke 316 — *
Bonby 447 — 8 C2
Boston 26,591 — 11 F3
Boothby Graffoe 189 — 10 C1
Boothby Pagnell 108 — 10 C4
Bottesford 11,702 — 8 B3
Boultham 6,415 — 8 C6
Bourne 9,988 — 10 D5
Braceborough & Wilsthorpe 253 — 10 D6
Bracebridge Heath 2,758 — 10 C1
Braceby & Sapperton 52 — 10 C4
Brackenborough with Little Grimsby 88 — *
Bradley 186 — 9 E3
Brampton 66 — 8 B5
Brandon — 10 B2
Bransby — 8 B5
Branston & Mere 3,655 — 10 C1
Brant Broughton & Stragglethorpe 671 — 10 B2
Bratoft 158 — 11 G1
Brattleby 88 — 8 C5
Brauncewell 570 — *
Bridge End — 10 D4
Brigg 5,322 — 8 C3
Brigsley 353 — 9 E3
Brinkhill 76 — 9 F6
Broadholme 110 — 8 B6
Brocklesby 150 — 8 D2
Brothertoft -with- Holland Fen 586 — 11 E3
Broughton 4,448 — 8 C3
Broxholme 56 — 8 B6
Brumby — 8 B3
Bucknall 295 — 9 E6
Bulby — 10 D4
Bullington 39 — *
Burgh le Marsh 2,001 — 11 H1
Burgh on Bain 104 — 9 E5
Burnham — 8 D2
Burringham 1,169 — 8 B3
Burton 192 — 8 C6
Burton-le-Coggles 120 — 10 C4
Burton Pedwardine 105 — 10 D3
Burton upon Stather 2,719 — 8 B2
Burwell 66 — 9 F5
Buslingthorpe 74 — *
Butterwick 1,020 — 11 G3
Butterwick 827 — 8 D3
Cabourne 86 — 8 D3
Cadney 454 — 8 C3
Caenby 104 — *
Caistor 2,502 — 8 D3
Calcethorpe with Kelstern 51 — 9 E4
Cammeringham 92 — 8 C5
Candlesby with Gunby 147 — 11 G1
Canwick 204 — 8 C6
Careby Aunby & Holywell 157 — 10 C5
Carlby 244 — 10 C6
Carlton-le-Moorland 407 — 10 B1
Carlton Scroop 178 — 10 C3
Carrington 486 — 11 F2
Castle Bytham 602 — 10 C5
Cawthorpe — 10 D5
Caythorpe 1,085 — 10 C2
Chain Bridge — 11 F3
Chapel Hill — 11 E2

Chapel St Leonards 2,884 — 9 H6
Chapelgate — 11 G5
Cherry Willingham 2,854 — 8 C6
Church End — 9 G4
Claxby 209 — 8 D4
Claxby 40 — 9 G6
Claxby with Moorby 43 — 11 F1
Claypole 741 — 10 B2
Claythorpe 20 — *
Cleethorpes 34,722 — 9 F3
Cold Hanworth 30 — 8 C5
Coleby — 8 B2
Coleby 440 — 10 C1
Colsterworth 1,452 — 10 B5
Coningsby 2,901 — 11 E2
Conisholme 52 — 9 G4
Corby Glen 607 — 10 C5
Corringham 429 — 8 B4
Counthorpe & Creeton 116 — 10 C5
Covenham St Bartholomew 179 — 9 F4
Covenham St Mary 117 — 9 F4
Cowbit 665 — 11 E5
Cranwell & Byard's Leap 1,915 — 10 C2
Creeton & Counthorpe 116 — 10 C5
Croft 717 — 11 H1
Crosby 7,661 — 8 B2
Crowland 3,292 — 11 E6
Crowle 3,699 — 8 A2
Croxby — 9 E4
Croxton 42 — 8 D2
Culverthorpe & Kelby 92 — 10 C3
Cumberworth 127 — 9 H6
Cuxwold — 9 E3
Dalby 37 — *
Dalderby — 11 E1
Dawsmere — 11 G4
Deeping St James 6,285 — 11 E6
Deeping St Nicholas 1,236 — 11 E5
Denton 282 — 10 B4
Derrythorpe — 8 B3
Digby 511 — 10 D2
Doddington & Whisby 303 — 8 B6
Dogdyke 368 — 11 E2
Donington 2,569 — 11 E4
Donington on Bain 298 — 9 E5
Dorrington 339 — 10 D2
Dowsby 215 — 10 D4
Driby — 9 G6
Dry Doddington & Westborough 272 — 10 B2
Dunholme 1,469 — 8 C5
Dunsby 110 — 10 D4
Dunston 677 — 10 D1
Dyke — 10 D5
Eagle & Swinethorpe 769 — 10 B1
Eagle Moor — 10 B1
Ealand — 8 A2
East Barkwith 331 — 9 E5
East Ferry 96 — 8 B4
East Halton 617 — 8 D2
East Heckington — 11 E3
East Keal 324 — 11 F1
East Kirkby 271 — 11 F1
East Lound — 8 A3
East Ravendale 97 — 9 E4
East Stockwith 239 — 8 A4
East Torrington — 9 E5
Eastoft 393 — 8 A2
Easton 90 — 10 B4
Eastville 243 — 11 G2
Edenham 335 — 10 D5
Edlington with Wispington 125 — 9 E6
Elkington 271 — 9 F4
Elsham 380 — 8 C2
Epworth 340 — 8 A3

Ewerby & Evedon 332 — 10 D3
Faldingworth 239 — 8 D5
Farlesthorpe 56 — 9 G6
Fenton 244 — 8 B6
Fenton 82 — 10 B2
Ferriby Sluice — 8 C2
Fillingham 151 — 8 C5
Firsby 229 — 11 G1
Fishtoft 5,198 — 11 F3
Fishtoft Drove — 11 F2
Fiskerton 955 — 8 D6
Fleet 1,710 — 11 F5
Fleet Hargate — 11 G5
Flixborough 946 — 8 B2
Fockerby & Garthorpe 362 — 8 B2
Folkingham 438 — 10 D4
Fosdyke 486 — 11 F4
Foston 429 — 10 B3
Fotherby 426 — 9 F4
Frampton 1,343 — 11 F3
Freiston 1,106 — 11 F3
Friesthorpe 66 — 8 D5
Friskney 1,372 — 11 G2
Friskney Fairdyke — 11 G2
Friskney Tofts — 11 G2
Frith Bank — 11 F2
Frithville 531 — 11 F2
Fulbeck 483 — 10 C2
Fulletby 76 — 9 F6
Fulnetby 14 — 8 D5
Fulstow 527 — 9 F4
Gainsborough 17,851 — 8 B4
Garthorpe & Fockerby 362 — 8 B2
Gate Burton 61 — 8 B5
Gautby 47 — 9 E6
Gayton le Marsh 140 — 9 G5
Gayton le Wold 58 — *
Gedney 1,952 — 11 G5
Gedney Broadgate — 11 G5
Gedney Drove End — 11 G4
Gedney Dyke — 11 G5
Gedney Hill 576 — 11 F6
Gibraltar — 11 H1
Gipsey Bridge — 11 F2
Glentham 325 — 8 C4
Glentworth 361 — 8 C5
Goltho 64 — *
Gosberton 2,678 — 11 E4
Goulceby 130 — 9 E6
Goxhill 1,796 — 8 D1
Goxhill Haven — 8 D1
Graby — 10 D4
Grainsby 48 — 9 F4
Grainthorpe 684 — 9 F4
Graizelound — 8 A4
Grange de Lings 44 — *
Grantham 32,083 — 10 B4
Grasby 388 — 8 D3
Grayingham 85 — 8 C4
Great Carlton 129 — 9 G5
Great Coates — 9 E3
Great Gonerby 1,630 — 10 B3
Great Hale 580 — 10 D3
Great Limber 276 — *
Great Ponton 287 — 10 B4
Great Steeping 221 — 11 G1
Great Sturton 40 — 9 E6
Greatford 249 — 10 D6
Greetham with Somersby 136 — 9 F6
Grimoldby 951 — 9 G5
Grimsby 90,517 — 9 F2
Grimsthorpe — 10 C5
Gunby & Stainby 146 — 10 B5
Gunness 2,495 — 8 B2
Guy's Head — 11 G5
Habrough 652 — 8 D2
Haconby 359 — 10 D5
Hackthorn 192 — 8 C5
Hagworthingham 269 — 9 F6
Hainton 115 — 9 E5
Hallington 40 — 9 F5
Halltoft End — 11 F3
Haltham 116 — 11 E1
Halton Fenside — 11 G1
Halton Holegate 417 — 11 G1
Hameringham 61 — 11 F1

Hannah cum Hagnaby 71 — 9 H5
Hanthorpe — 10 D5
Hardwick 35 — *
Hareby — 11 F1
Harlaxton 757 — 10 B4
Harmston 292 — 10 C1
Harpswell 107 — 8 C4
Harrington 25 — 9 F6
Hatcliffe 107 — 9 E3
Hatton 116 — 9 E6
Haugh 13 — *
Haugham 37 — 9 F5
Hawerby cum Beesby 23 — *
Hawthorpe — 10 C4
Haxey 4,050 — 8 A3
Healing 1,979 — 9 E3
Heapham 95 — 8 B5
Heckington 2,215 — 10 D3
Hedgehog Bridge — 11 E3
Heighington 2,271 — 8 C6
Helpringham 739 — 10 D3
Hemingby 224 — 9 E6
Hemswell 842 — 8 B4
Hemswell Cliff — 8 B4
Heydour 244 — 10 C3
Hibaldstow 1,899 — 8 C3
High Ferry — 11 F2
High Toynton 69 — 9 F6
Hilldyke — 11 F2
Hogsthorpe 797 — 9 H6
Holbeach 8,180 — 11 F4
Holbeach Bank — 11 F4
Holbeach Drove — 11 F6
Holbeach Hurn — 11 G4
Holbeach St Johns — 11 F5
Holbeach St Matthew — 11 G4
Holdingham — 10 D3
Holland Fen-with-Brothertoft 586 — 11 E3
Holme 101 — *
Holton cum Beckering 119 — 8 D5
Holton le Clay 3,818 — 9 F3
Holton le Moor 188 — 8 D4
Honington 129 — 10 C3
Horbling 383 — 10 D4
Horkstow 90 — 8 C2
Horncastle 4,994 — 9 E6
Horsington 234 — 9 E6
Hough-on-the-Hill 346 — 10 B3
Hougham 198 — 10 B3
Howell — 10 D3
Howsham — 8 C3
Hubbert's Bridge — 11 E3
Humberston 5,514 — 9 F3
Humby — 10 C4
Hundleby 416 — 11 F1
Huttoft 479 — 9 H6
Immingham 11,138 — 9 E2
Ingham 66 — 8 C5
Ingoldmells 1,668 — 9 H6
Ingoldsby 270 — 10 C4
Irby upon Humber 128 — 9 E3
Irby in the Marsh 168 — 11 G1
Irnham 141 — 10 C4
Keadby with Althorpe 1,733 — 8 B3
Keal Cotes — 11 F1
Keddington 91 — *
Keelby 2,311 — 9 E3
Kelby — 10 C3
Kelstern with Calcethorpe 51 — 9 E4
Kettlethorpe 396 — 8 B6
Kexby 325 — 8 B5
Killingholme (North) 267 — 8 D2
Killingholme (South) 1,140 — 8 D2
Kirby — 8 D4
Kirkby Green — 10 D1
Kirkby la Thorpe 384 — 10 D3
Kirkby on Bain 308 — 11 E1
Kirkby Underwood 159 — 10 D4

Kirmington **331** 8 D2
Kirmond le Mire **43** 9 E4
Kirton **3,798** 11 F3
Kirton Holme 11 E3
Kirton in Lindsey **2,773** 8 C4
Kirton End 11 F3
Knaith **248** 8 B5
Laceby **2,666** 9 E3
Lade Bank 11 G2
Langrick 11 E2
Langriville **412** *
Langtoft **1,108** 10 D6
Langton **39** 9 E6
Langton by Spilsby **62** 9 G6
Langton by Wragby **94** 8 D6
Langworth 8 D6
Laughterton 8 B6
Laughton **326** 8 B4
Lea **958** 8 B5
Leadenham **410** 10 C2
Leake Commonside 11 F2
Leake Hurn's End 11 G2
Leasingham **1,650** 10 D2
Legbourne **596** 9 F5
Legsby **231** 8 D5
Lenton Keisby & Osgodby **162** 10 C4
Leverton **3,798** 11 G2
Leverton Lucasgate 11 G2
Leverton Outgate 11 G2
Lincoln **75,572** 8 C6
Linwood **105** 8 D5
Lissington **171** 8 D5
Little Bytham **265** 10 C5
Little Carlton **106** 9 G5
Little Cawthorpe **133** 9 F5
Little Hale **149** 10 D3
Little London 11 E5
Little Ponton & Stroxton **170** *
Little Steeping **149** 11 G1
Little Sutton **143** *
Londonthorpe & Harrowby Without **3,582** 10 C3
Long Bennington **1,527** 10 B3
Long Sutton **3,779** 11 G5
Louth **14,348** 9 F5
Low Burnham 8 A3
Low Toynton **21** *
Ludborough **214** 9 F4
Ludford **385** 9 E5
Luddington & Haldenby **360** 8 B2
Lusby with Winceby **99** 11 F1
Lutton **1,016** 11 G4
Mablethorpe & Sutton **10,253** 9 H5
Maidenwell **53** *
Maltby le Marsh **338** 9 G5
Manby **739** 9 G5
Manton **124** 8 C3
Mareham le Fen **818** 11 E1
Mareham on the Hill **88** 11 E1
Markby **64** 9 G5
Market Deeping **5,351** 10 D6
Market Rasen **2,948** 8 D4
Market Stainton **37** 9 E5
Marshchapel **677** 9 F4
Marston **359** 10 B3
Martin **749** 10 D1
Martin Dales 11 E1
Marton **508** 8 B5
Mavis Enderby **72** 11 F1
Medlam 11 F2
Melton Ross **197** 8 D3
Messingham **2,952** 8 B3
Metheringham **2,700** 10 D1
Middle Rasen **1,370** 8 D4
Midville **177** 11 F2
Millthorpe 10 D4
Minting **223** 9 E6
Moorby 11 F1
Moortown 8 D4
Morton **1,108** 8 A4
Morton **1,417** 10 D5
Moulton **3,025** 11 F5
Moulton Chapel 11 F5
Moulton Seas End 11 F4
Muckton **31** 9 F5
Mumby **348** 9 H6
Navenby **1,165** 10 C1
Nettleham **3,152** 8 C6
Nettleton **604** 8 D4
New Bolingbroke 11 F1
New Holland **872** 8 D1
New Leake **330** 11 G2
New Waltham **3,623** 9 F3
New York 11 E2
Newball **44** *
Newtoft 8 C5
Newton by Toft 8 D5
Newton & Haceby **43** 10 D3
Newton on Trent **261** 8 B6
Nocton **592** 10 D1
Normanby 8 B2
Normanby by Spital **266** 8 C5
Normanby le Wold **73** 8 D4
Normanton **93** 10 C3
North Carlton **133** 8 C6
North Coates **470** 9 F3
North Cockerington **224** 9 F4
North Elkington 9 F4
North Greetwell **370** 8 C6
North Hykeham **10,506** 10 C1
North Kelsey **922** 8 C3
North Kyme **493** 10 D2
North Ormsby **52** 9 F4
North Owersby **283** 8 D4
North Rauceby **137** 10 C3
North Scarle **484** 10 B1
North Somercotes **1,506** 9 G4
North Thoresby **1,271** 9 F4
North Willingham **131** 9 E5
North Witham **166** 10 B5
Northgate 11 E4
Northlands 11 F2
Northorpe **142** 8 B4
Northorpe 10 D5
Norton Disney **232** 10 B1
Oasby 10 C3
Old Bolingbroke 11 F1
Old Leake **1,569** 11 G2
Old Somerby **229** 10 C4
Orby **323** 11 G1
Osbournby **296** 10 D3
Osgodby **514** 8 D4
Owmby-by-Spital **294** 8 C5
Owston Ferry **1,138** 8 A3
Oxcombe 9 F6
Partney **238** 9 G6
Pickworth **106** 10 C4
Pilham **64** 8 B4
Pinchbeck **4,925** 11 E5
Pinchbeck West 11 E5
Pode Hole 11 E5
Pointon & Sempringham **443** 10 D4
Potterhanworth **562** 10 D1
Quadring **1,029** 11 E4
Quadring Eaudike 11 E4
Quarrington 10 D3
Raithby **168** 11 F1
Raithby cum Maltby **50** 9 F5
Ranby **50** *
Rand **58** 8 D6
Redbourne **328** 8 C4
Reepham **816** 8 D6
Revesby **233** 11 F1
Riby **153** 9 E3
Rigsby with Ailby **27** *
Rippingale **677** 10 D4
Risby cum Roxby **440** 8 B2
Risegate 11 E4
Riseholme **137** *
Ropsley & Humby **725** 10 C4
Rothwell **202** 8 D4
Roughton **507** 11 E1
Rowston **128** 10 D2
Roxby cum Risby **440** 8 B2
Roxholm **78** *
Ruckland 9 F6
Ruskington **3,954** 10 D2
Saleby with Beesby **235** 9 G6
Salmonby 9 F6
Saltfleet 9 G4
Saltfleetby All Saints **106** 9 G4
Saltfleetby St Clements **67** 9 G4
Saltfleetby St Peter **349** 9 G5
Sandholme 11 F3
Sandilands 9 H5
Sandtoft 8 A3
Santon 8 C2
Saracen's Head 11 F4
Sausthorpe **112** 9 F6
Saxby **36** 8 C5
Saxby All Saints **218** 8 C2
Saxilby with Ingleby **3,086** 8 B6
Scamblesby **239** 9 F6
Scampton **1,322** 8 C5
Scartho 9 A3
Scawby **2,404** 8 C3
Scopwick **996** 10 D1
Scothern **741** 8 C6
Scotter **2,670** 8 B3
Scotterthorpe 8 B3
Scotton **578** 8 B4
Scrane End 11 F3
Scredington **239** 10 D3
Scremby 11 G1
Scrivelsby **35** *
Scrub Hill 11 E2
Scunthorpe **46,456** 8 B3
Seacroft 11 H1
Searby cum Owmby **170** 8 D3
Seathorne 11 H1
Sedgebrook **302** 10 B3
Sibsey **1,403** 11 F2
Sibsey Fen Side 11 F2
Silk Willoughby **304** 10 D3
Sixhills **53** 9 E5
Skegness **16,355** 11 H1
Skeldyke 11 F3
Skellingthorpe **3,162** 8 B6
Skendleby **155** 9 G6
Skidbrooke with Saltfleet Haven **524** 9 G4
Skillington **236** 10 B4
Sleaford **10,388** 10 D3
Sloothby & Willoughby **534** 9 G6
Snarford **45** *
Snelland **81** 8 D5
Snitterby **228** 8 C4
Somerby **16** *
Somersby 9 F6
Sots Hole 10 D1
Sotby **61** 9 E6
South Carlton **86** 8 C6
South Cockerington **220** 9 F5
South Elkington 9 F5
South End 8 D2
South Ferriby **614** 8 C2
South Hykeham 10 C1
South Kelsey **514** 8 C4
South Kyme **284** 11 E2
South Ormsby cum Ketsby **85** 9 F6
South Reston **215** 9 G5
South Rauceby **335** 10 C3
South Somercotes **222** 9 G4
South Thoresby **90** 9 G6
South Willingham **150** 9 E5
South Witham **1,171** 10 B5
Southrey 10 D1
Spalding **19,561** 11 E5
Spanby 10 D3
Spilsby **1,908** 11 G1
Spridlington **164** 8 C5
Springthorpe **126** 8 B5
Stainby & Gunby **146** 10 B5
Stainfield **99** 8 D6
Stainfield 10 D5
Stainton by Langworth **82** 8 D6
Stainton le Vale **259** 9 E4
Stallingborough **943** 9 E2
Stamford **13,566** 10 C6
Stapleford **79** 10 B2
Stenigot **38** *
Stewton **82** 9 F5
Stickford **400** 11 F1
Stickney **953** 11 F2
Stixwould & Woodhall **242** 11 E1
Stoke Rochford **147** 10 B4
Stow **340** 8 B5
Stroxton & Little Ponton **170** *
Strubby with Woodthorpe **131** 9 G5
Stubton **133** 10 B2
Sturton by Stow **1,080** 8 B5
Sudbrooke **1,399** 8 C6
Sudbrooke 10 C3
Surfleet **1,127** 11 E4
Surfleet Seas End 11 F4
Susworth 8 B3
Sutterton **1,202** 11 F3
Sutton Bridge **3,457** 11 G5
Sutton Crosses 11 G5
Sutton St Edmund **581** 11 F6
Sutton St James **94** 11 G5
Sutton on Sea & Mablethorpe **10,253** 9 H5
Swaby **200** 9 F6
Swallow **193** 9 E3
Swaton **169** 10 D3
Swayfield **276** 10 C5
Swinderby **598** 10 B1
Swineshead **2,057** 11 E3
Swineshead Bridge 11 E3
Swinhope **117** 9 E4
Swinstead **246** 10 C5
Syston **133** 10 B3
Tallington **264** 10 D6
Tathwell **171** 9 F5
Tattershall **2,225** 11 E1
Tattershall Bridge 11 E2
Tattershall Thorpe **246** 11 E1
Tealby **521** 9 E4
Temple Bruer with Temple High Grange **67** *
Tetford **414** 9 F6
Tetney **1,691** 9 F3
Tetney Lock 9 F3
Thealby 8 B2
Theddlethorpe All Saints **182** 9 G5
Theddlethorpe St Helen **422** 9 G5
Thimbleby **233** 9 E6
Thonock **30** *
Thoresway **91** 9 E4
Thorganby **44** 9 E4
Thornton 11 E1
Thornton Curtis **279** 8 D2
Thornton le Moor 8 D4
Thornton le Fen **336** *
Thorpe 9 G5
Thorpe on the Hill **506** 10 B1
Thorpe le Fallows **13** 8 B5
Thorpe Fendykes 11 G1
Thorpe St Peter **342** 11 G1
Threekingham **157** 10 D4
Thurlby 9 G6
Thurlby **1,566** 10 D5
Thurlby **754** 10 B1
Timberland **416** 10 D1
Toft next Newton **423** 8 D5
Toft with Lound & Manthorpe **258** 10 D5
Torksey **506** 8 B6
Toynton All Saints **349** 11 G1
Toynton Fen Side 11 F1
Toynton St Peter **248** 11 G1
Trusthorpe 9 H5
Tumby **203** *
Tumby Woodside 11 E2
Tupholme **21** *
Twenty 10 D5
Tydd Gote 11 G5
Tydd St Mary **87** 11 G5
Uffington **553** 10 D6
Ulceby **1,509** 8 D2
Ulceby with Fordington **131** 9 G6
Upton **386** 8 B5
Usselby 8 D4
Utterby **265** 9 F4
Waddingham **517** 8 C4
Waddington **5,393** 10 C1
Waddingworth **4** *
Wainfleet Bank 11 G1
Wainfleet All Saints **1,239** 11 G1
Wainfleet St Mary **965** 11 H1
Waithe **27** *
Walcot near Folkingham **53** 10 D4
Walcott **464** 10 D2
Walesby **242** 8 D4
Walkerith **60** 8 A4
Walmsgate **28** *
Waltham **6,157** 9 E3
Washingborough **3,728** 8 C6
Welbourn **671** 10 C2
Welby **153** 10 C3
Well **75** 9 G6
Wellingore **698** 10 C2
Welton **2,871** 8 C5
Welton le Marsh **198** 9 G6
Welton le Wold **109** 9 E5
West Ashby **252** 9 E6
West Barkwith **73** *
West Deeping **250** 10 D6
West Fen **103** *
West Firsby **35** *
West Halton **334** 8 B2
West Keal **310** 11 F1
West Rasen **97** 8 D5
West Ravendale **23** *
West Torrington **81** 8 D5
Westborough & Dry Doddington **272** 10 B3
Westby 10 C4
Westgate 8 A3
Westhorpe 11 E4
Weston **1,560** 11 F5
Weston Hills 11 F5
Westville **48** *
Westwoodside 8 A3
Whaplode **2,619** 11 F5
Whaplode Drove 11 F6
Whaplode St Catherine 11 F5
Whitton **173** 8 B1
Wickenby **214** 8 D5
Wigtoft **471** 11 E3
Wildmore **470** *
Wildsworth **39** 8 A4
Willingham by Stow **501** 8 B5
Willoughby with Sloothby **534** 9 G6
Willoughton **314** 8 B4
Wilsford **384** 10 C3
Wilsthorpe & Braceborough **253** 10 D6
Winceby with Lusby **99** 9 F6
Winteringham **953** 8 B1
Winterton **4,895** 8 B2
Winthorpe 11 H1
Wispington with Edlington **125** 9 E6
Witham on the Hill **208** 10 D5
Withcall **62** *
Withern with Stain **415** 9 G5
Wold Newton **72** 9 E4
Wood Enderby **158** 11 E1
Woodhall Spa **2,958** 11 E1
Woolsthorpe **438** 10 B4
Woolsthorpe Colsterworth 10 B5
Wootton **392** 8 D2
Worlaby **480** 8 C2
Wragby **1,147** 8 D6
Wrangle **1,265** 11 G2
Wrangle Lowgate 11 G2
Wrawby **1,240** 8 C3
Wroot **403** 8 A3
Wyberton **3,906** 11 F3
Wyham cum Cadeby **29** *
Wyville cum Hungerton **56** 10 B5
Yarburgh **196** 9 F4

Population figures are based upon the 1991 census for Lincolnshire and relate to the local authority area or parish as constituted at that date. Population figures for North and North East Lincolnshire (formerly part of Humberside) are also included. Boundaries of the districts are shown on pages 4-5. Places with no population figure form part of a larger local authority area or parish.

Population figures in bold type.

*Place not included on map due to limitation of space

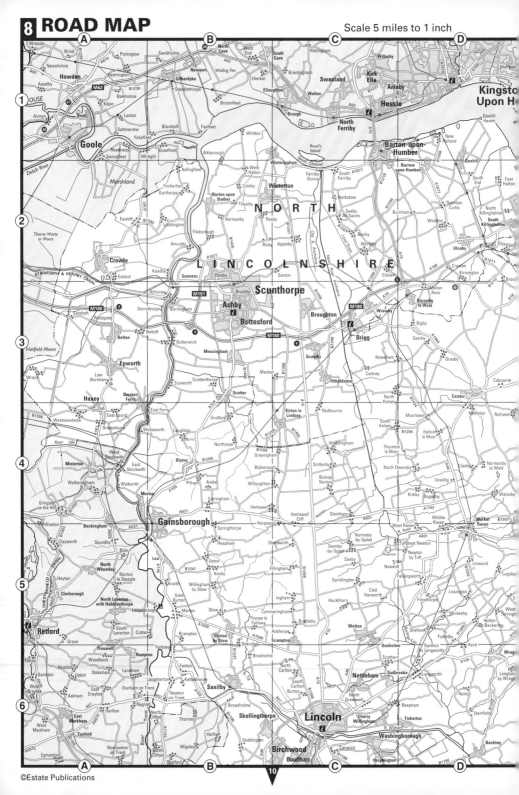

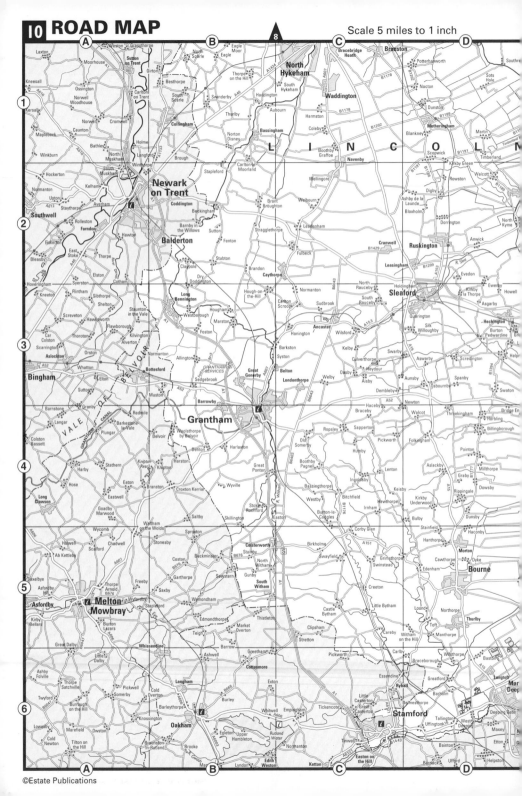

©Estate Publications

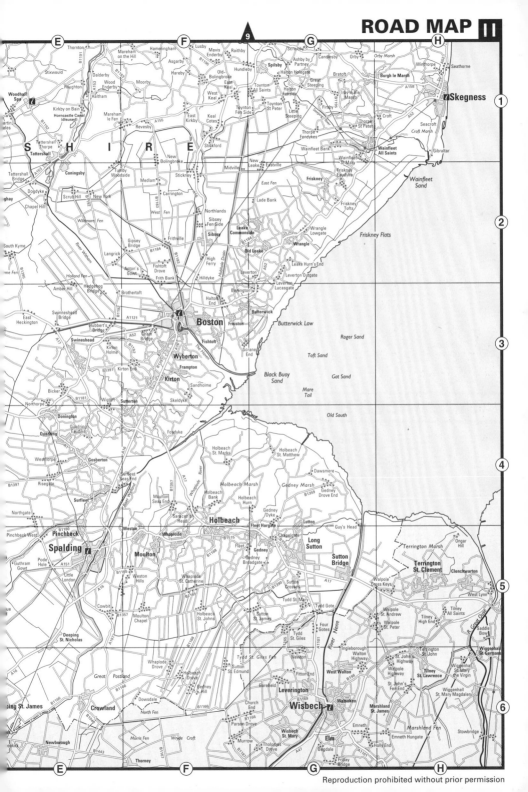

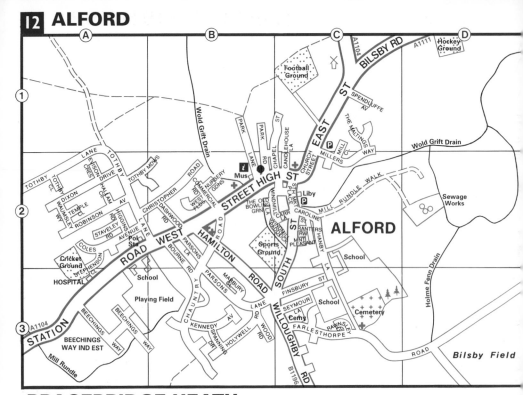

# BRACEBRIDGE HEATH

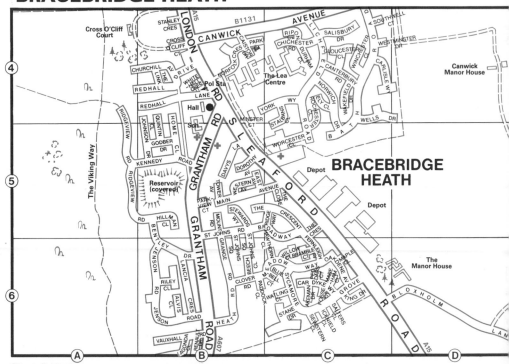

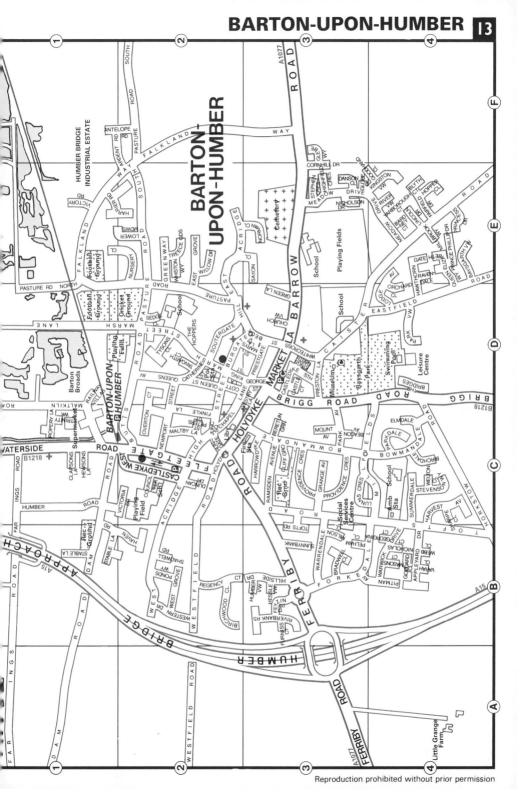

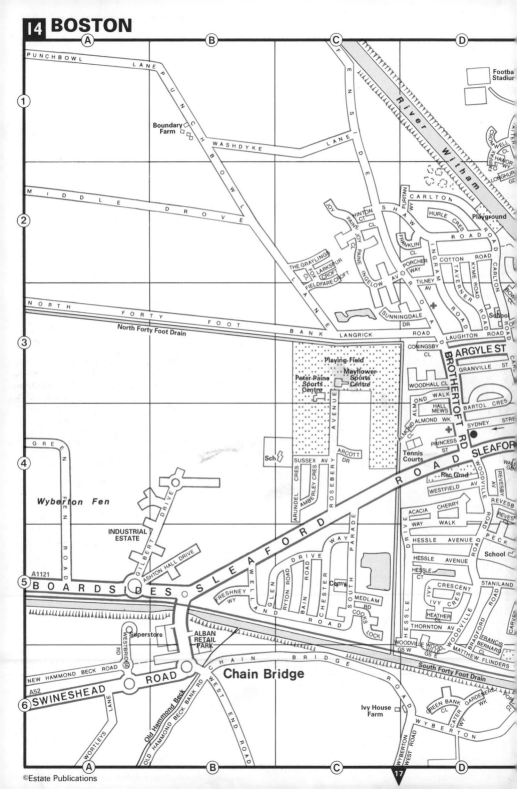

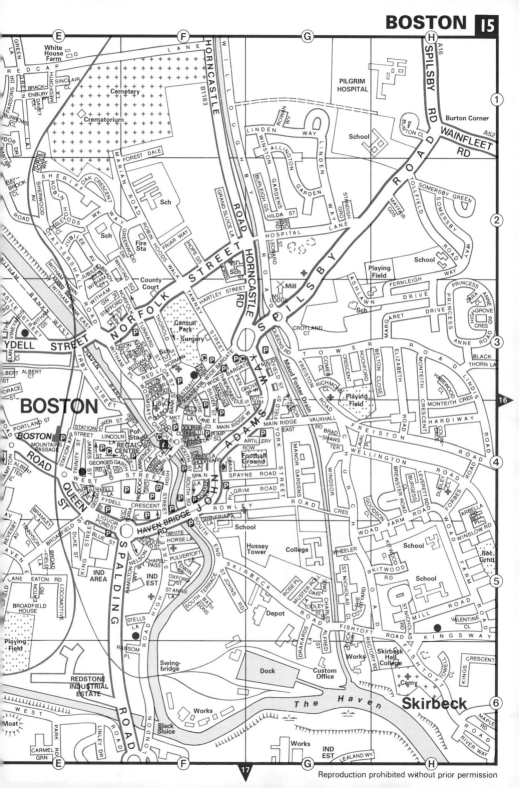

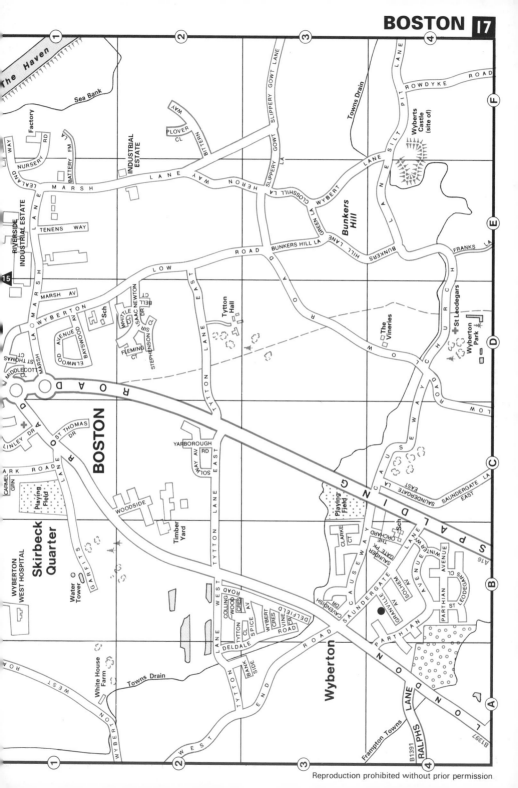

The Haven

Sea Bank

Factory

INDUSTRIAL ESTATE

RIVERSIDE INDUSTRIAL ESTATE

TENENS WAY

MARSH AV

WYBERTON

Sch

FLEMING CT

MIDDLECOTT CL

ST THOMAS CT

BOSTON

ROAD

LINLEY DR

St THOMAS DR

CARMEL GRN

PARK ROADE

Playing Field

Skirbeck Quarter

WYBERTON WEST HOSPITAL

Water Tower

GARFITS

White House Farm

Towns Drain

WOODSIDE

Timber Yard

YARBOROUGH RD

SOLWAY AV

TYTTON LANE EAST

TYTTON LANE WEST

DELDALE

COLLINGWOOD ROAD

TYTTON CL

SPICE AV

WYBERT CRES

DELFIELD ROAD

BANK SIDE

IRVINE CRES

CLARKE CT

THE ORCHARD

SAUNDERGATE PK

CAVENDISH DR

GRANVILLE DR

PARTHIAN AVENUE

SOLHEM AV

WINTERTON AVENUE

ST LEODEGARS CL

SAUNDERGATE LANE

SPALDING

SAUNDERGATE LA EAST

CAUSEWAY

Playing Field

Sch

NORTON LANE

RALPHS

Frampton Towns

B1391

B1397

A16

Wyberton

PLOVER CL

BITTERN WAY

MARSH LANE

HERON WAY

SLIPPERY GOWT LANE

SLIPPERY GOWT LA

CLOSSHILL LA

WYBERT

LOW ROAD

BUNKERS HILL LA

GREEN LA

HILL LANE

BUNKERS

WOOD ROAD

Tytton Hall

ISAAC NEWTON CT

WHITTLE CL

SIR STEPHENSON CT

Sch

ELMWOOD

BAYSWOOD

AVENUE

Towns Drain

LANE

PIT LANE

ROWDYKE ROAD

SILT LANE

Wyberts Castle (site of)

Bunkers Hill

St Leodegars

The Vineries

Wyberton Park

FRANKS LA

LOW

CHURCH ROAD

CAUSE WAY

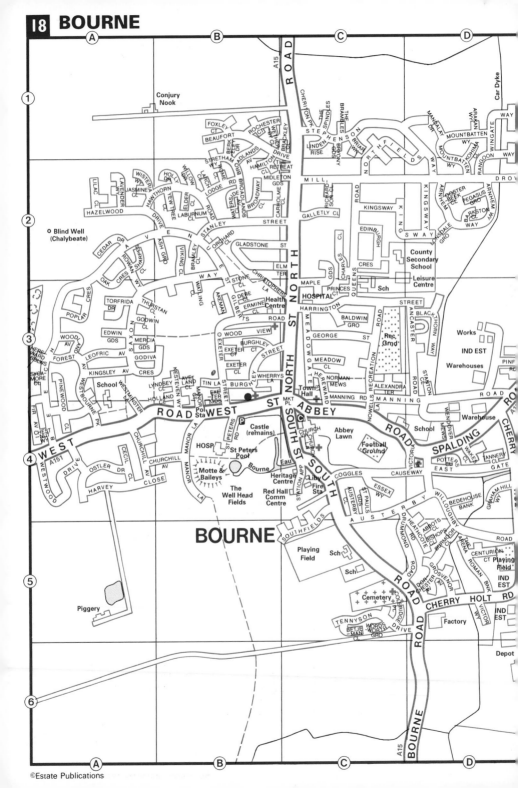

# 18 BOURNE

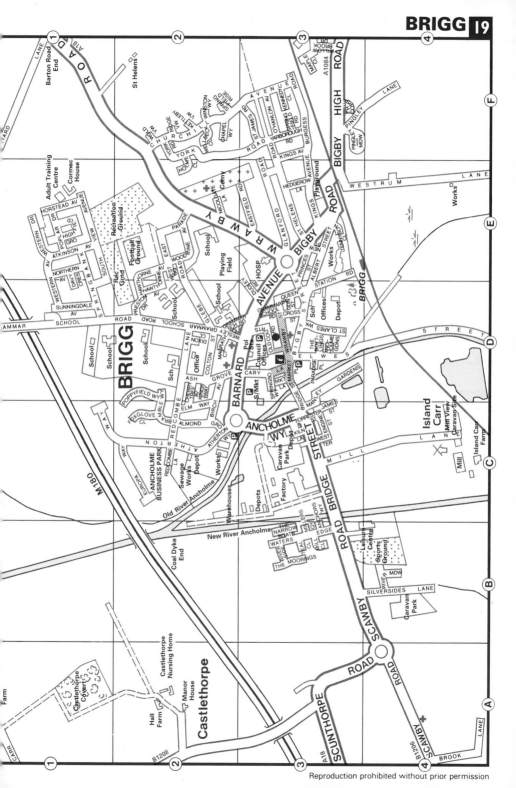

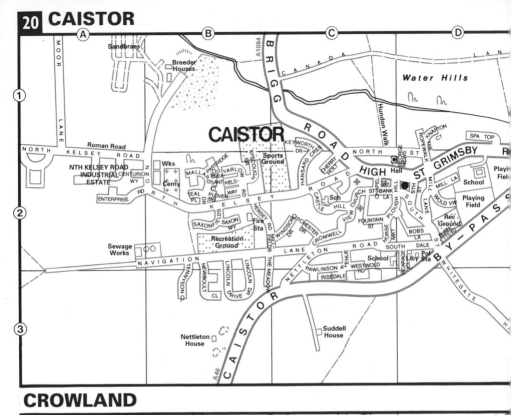

## CAISTOR

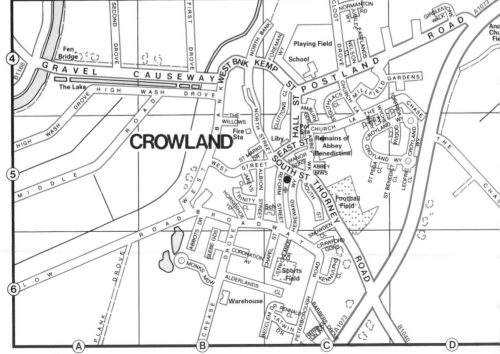

# CROWLAND

## CROWLAND

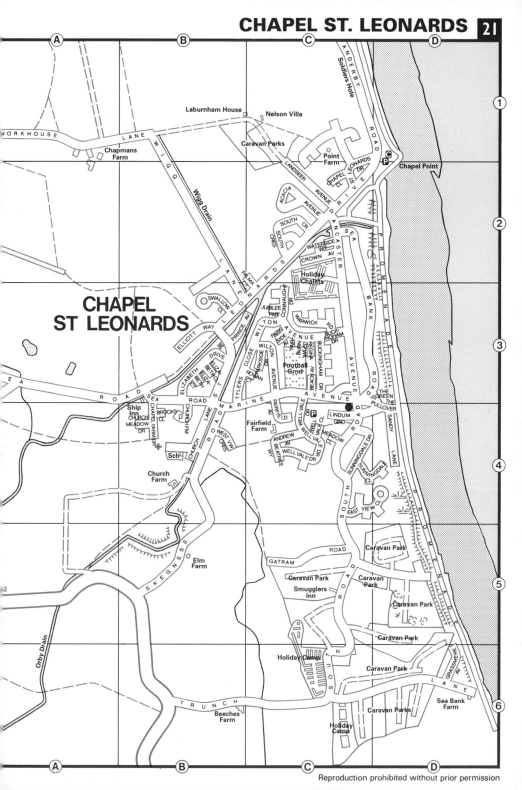

CLEETHORPES

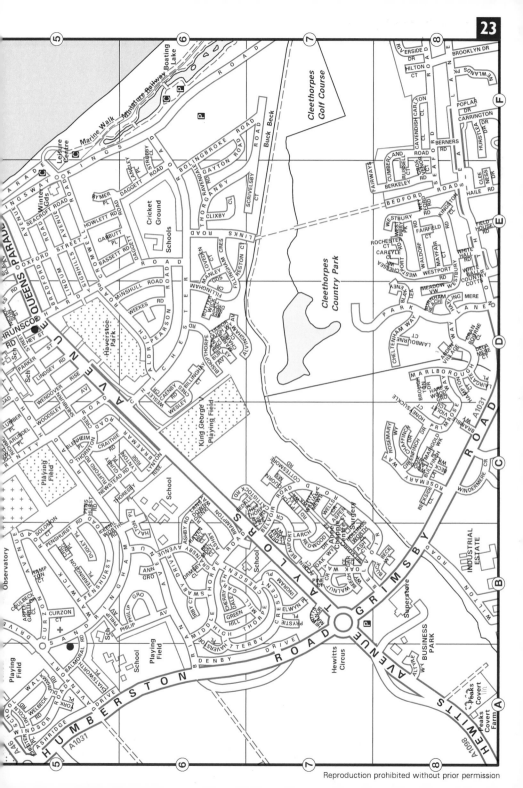

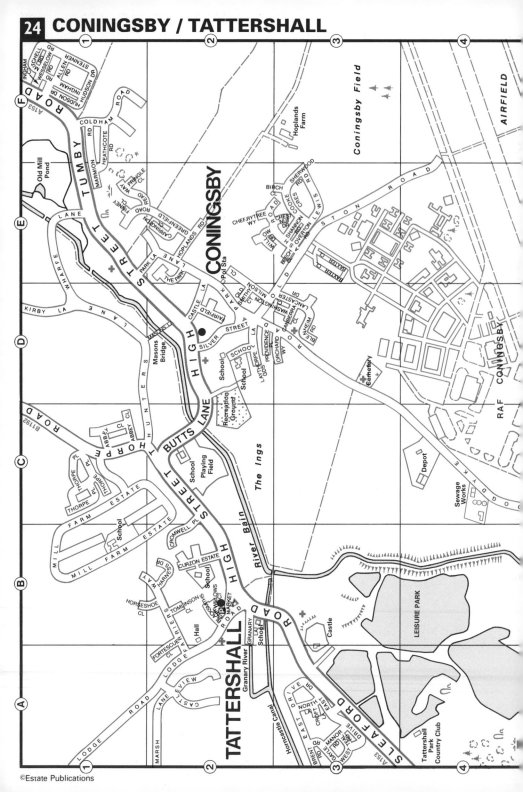

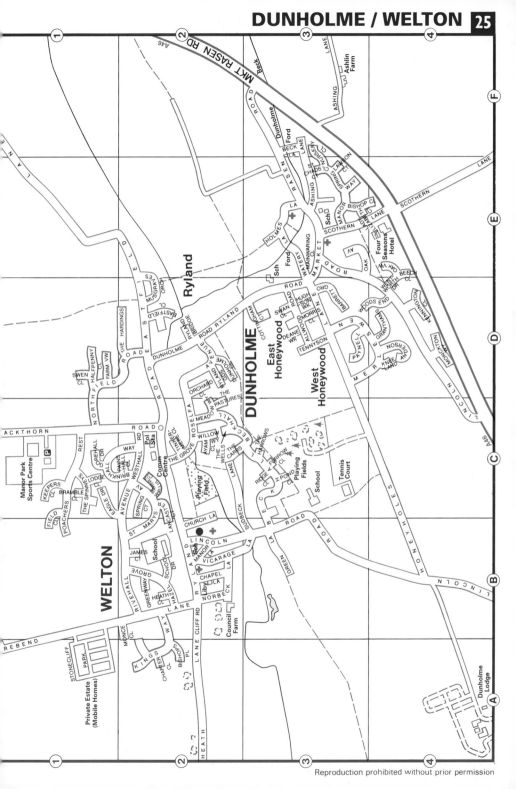

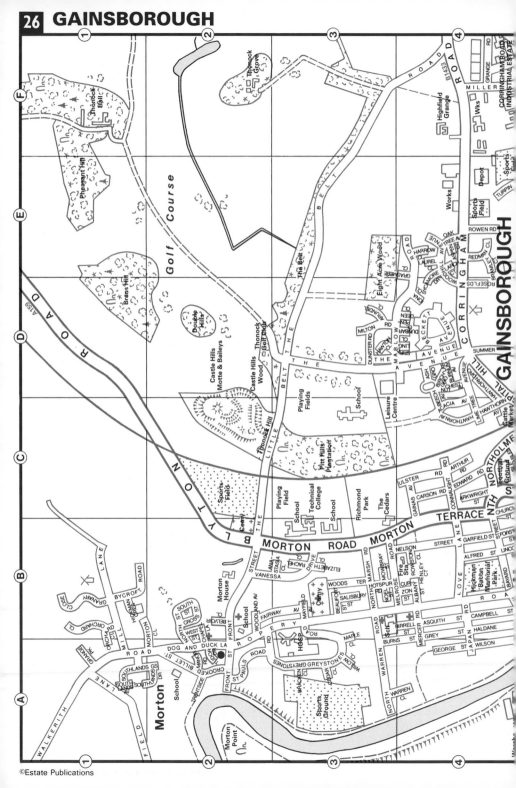

GAINSBOROUGH

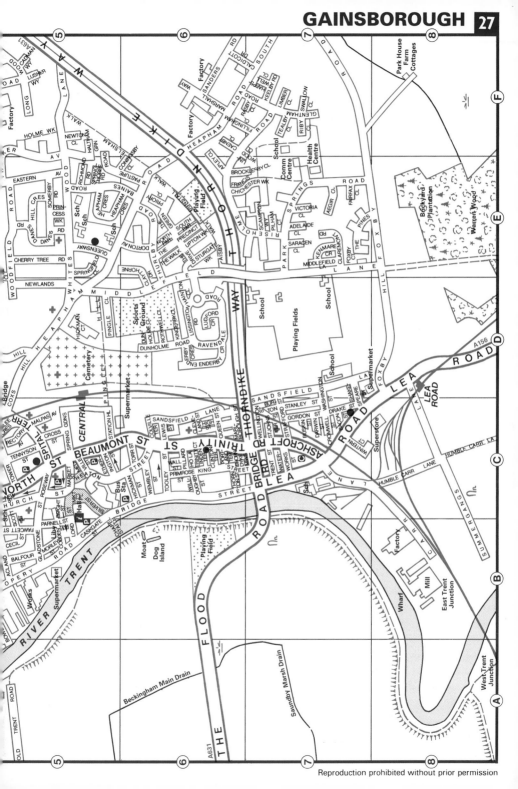

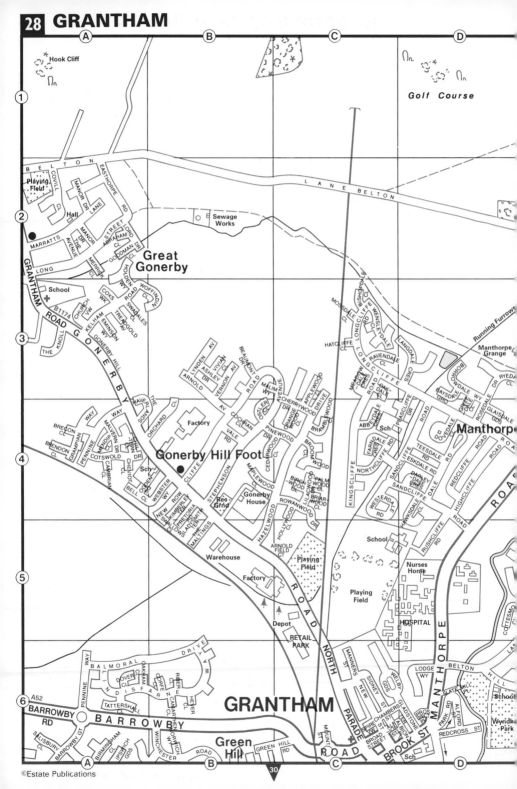

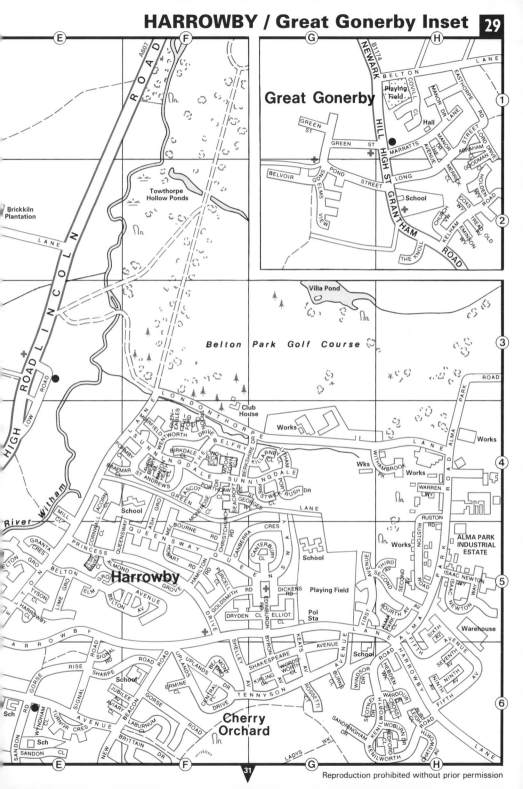

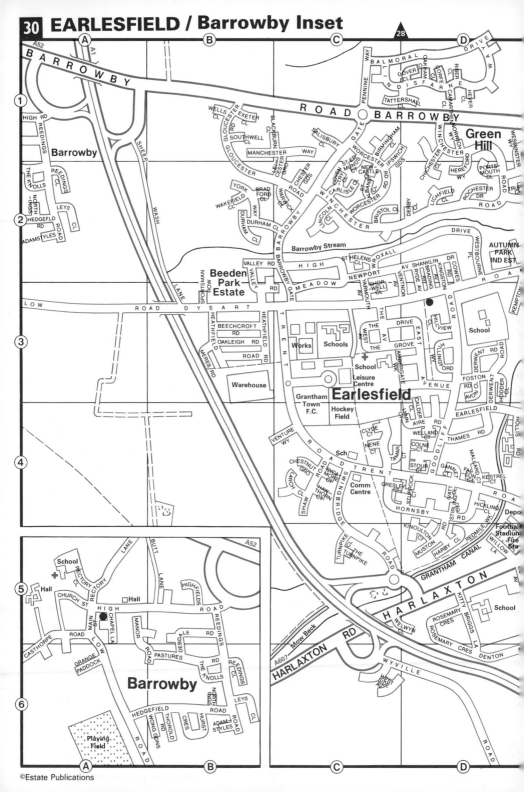

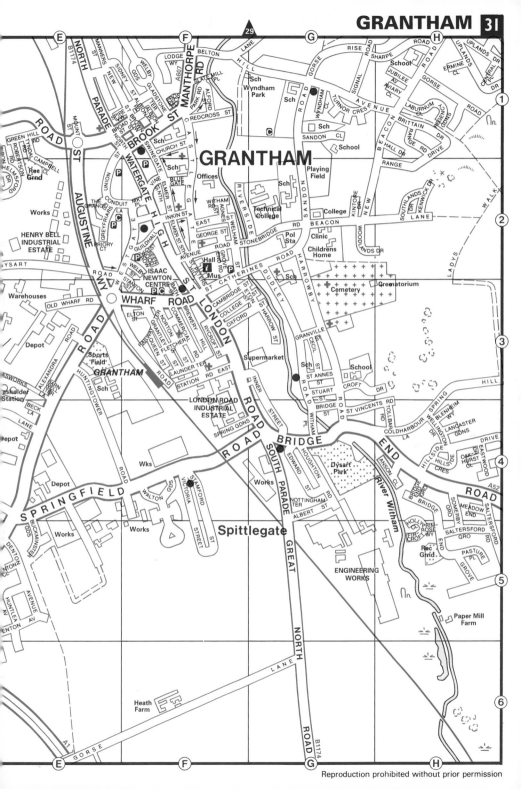

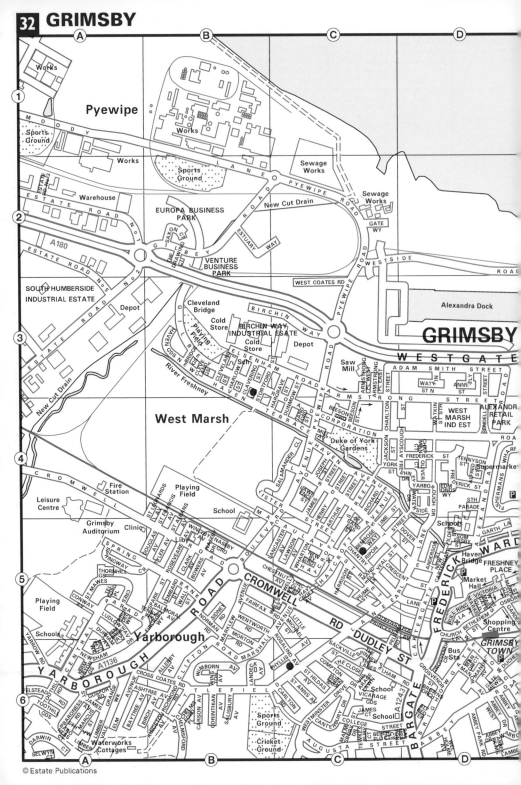

© Estate Publications

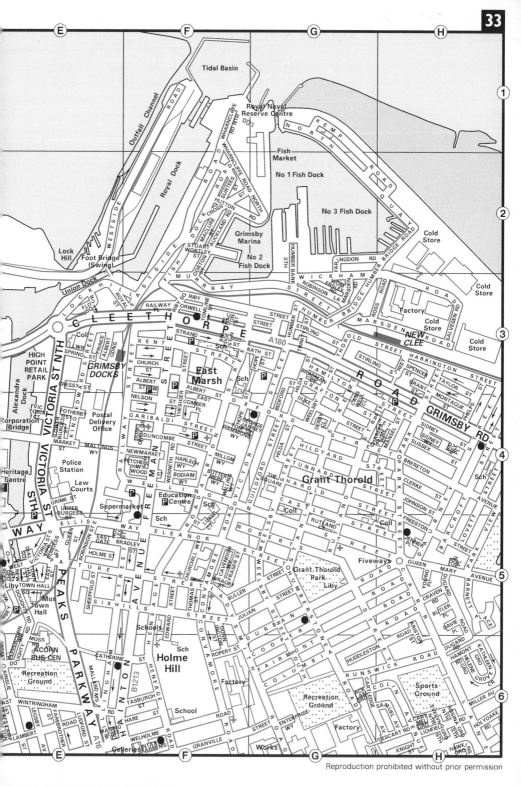

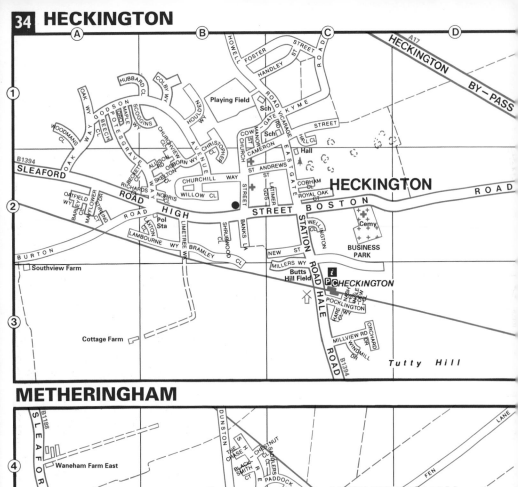

# METHERINGHAM

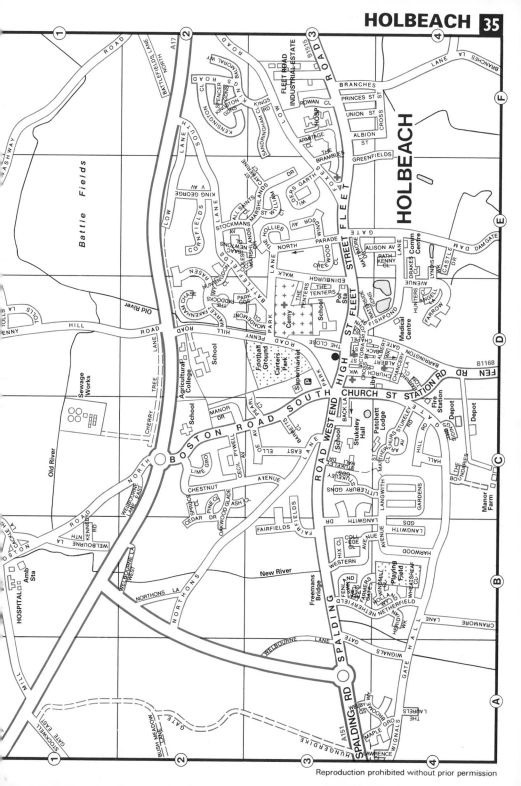

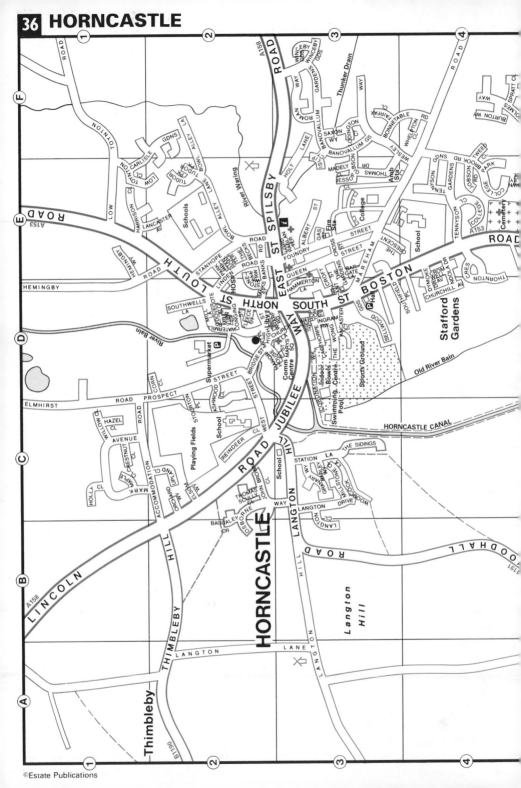

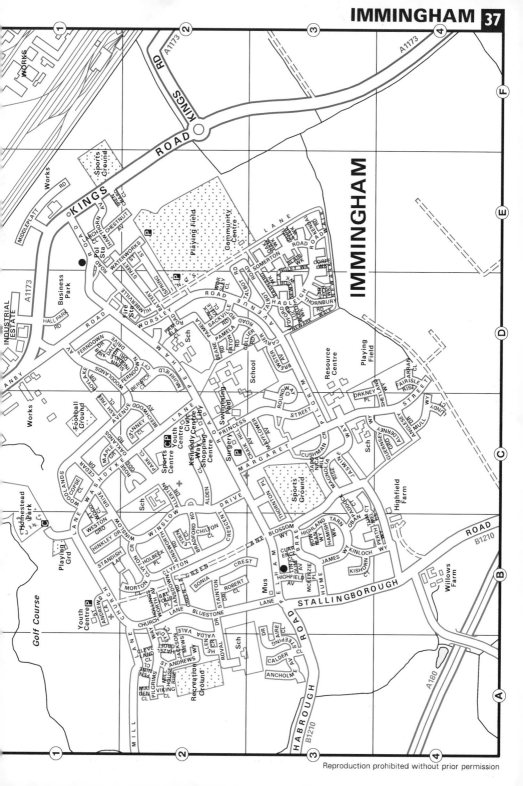

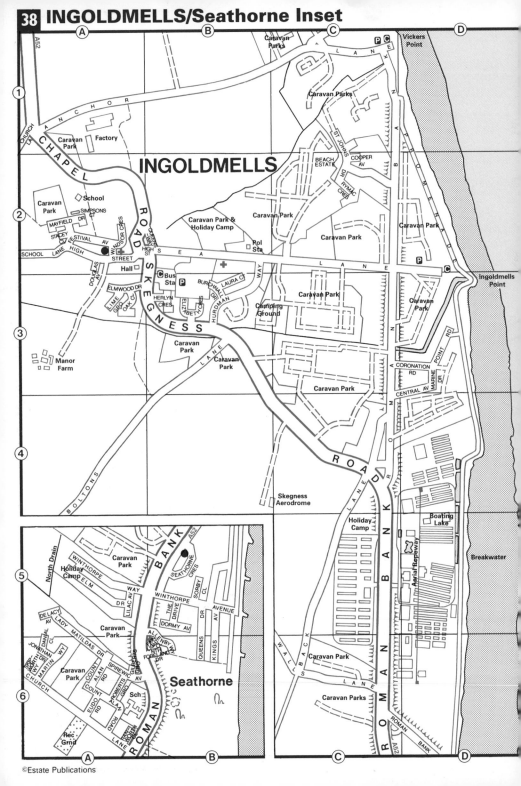

# 38 INGOLDMELLS/Seathorne Inset

INGOLDMELLS

Seathorne

©Estate Publications

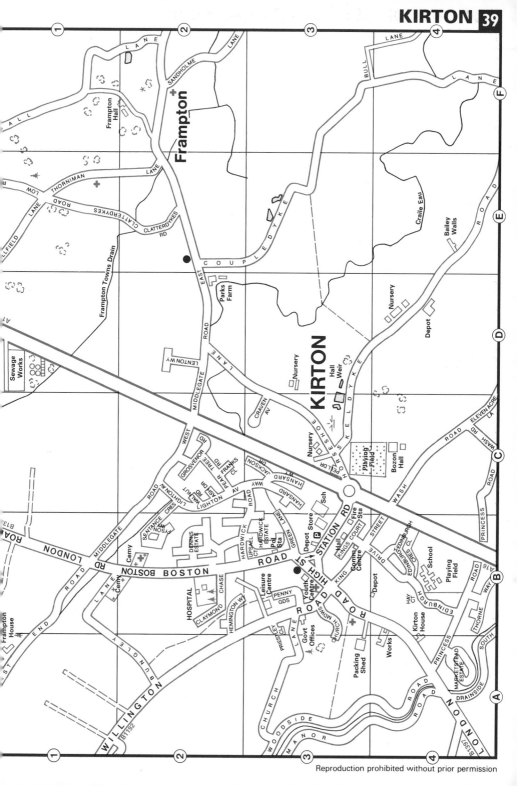

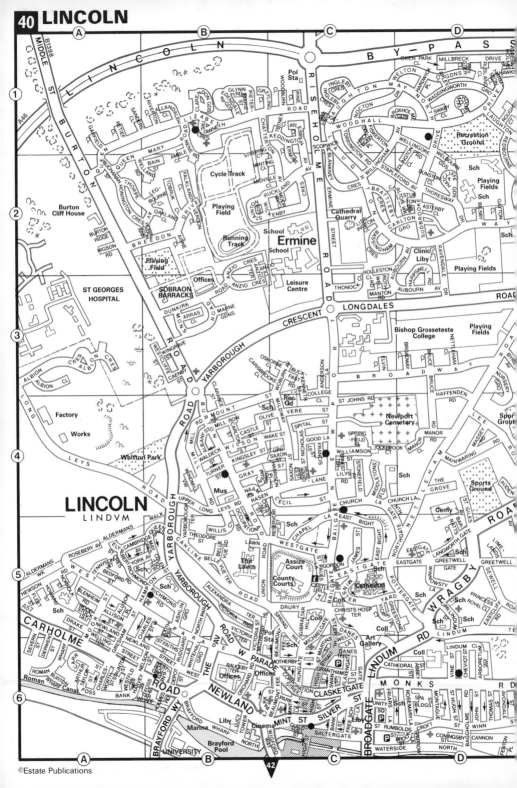

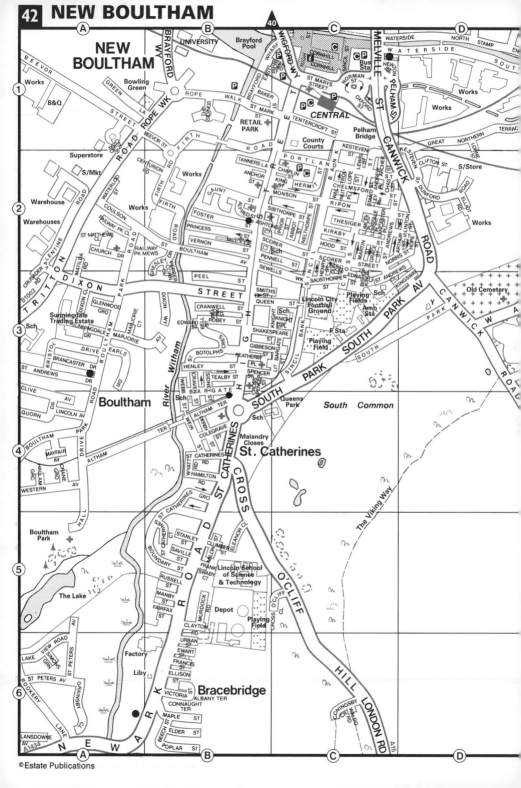

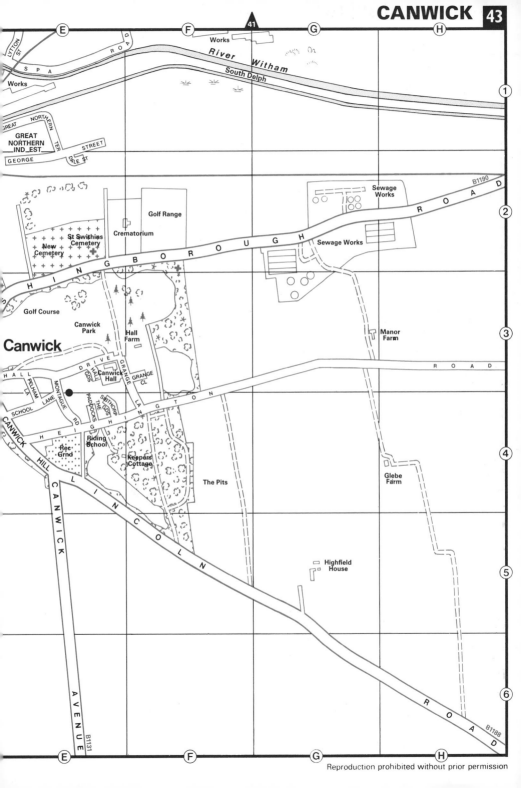

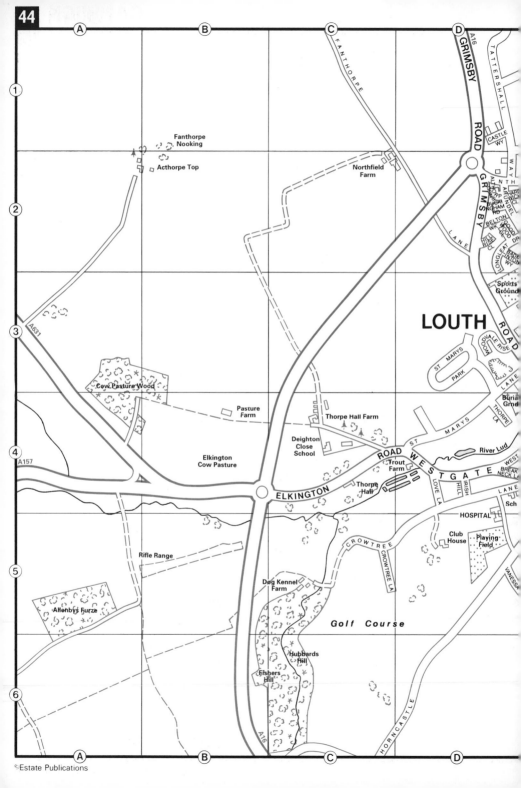

**44**

A B C D

1

2

Fanthorpe
Nooking

Acthorpe Top

Northfield
Farm

GRIMSBY ROAD A16

TATTERSHALL

CASTLE WY

GRIMSBY ROAD

ACTHORPE TOP
ARUNDEL
NTH
WK
BELTON WK
LONGLEAT WY

Sports
Ground

3

A631

Cow Pasture Wood

Pasture
Farm

Thorpe Hall Farm

Deighton
Close
School

LOUTH

ST MARYS PARK

OVALE RISE
BLOOM
THORPE LANE

Burial
Grnd

4

A157

Elkington
Cow Pasture

Trout
Farm

Thorpe
Hall

ROAD WESTGATE

ST MARYS

River Lud

WEST LANE

BREAK NECK LA

IRISH HILL

Sch

LOVE LA

HOSPITAL

ELKINGTON

Club
House

Playing
Field

VANESS

5

Rifle Range

Dog Kennel
Farm

CROWTREE LA

Allenbys Furze

*Golf Course*

6

Hubbards
Hill

Fishers
Hill

A16

HORNCASTLE

A B C D

©Estate Publications

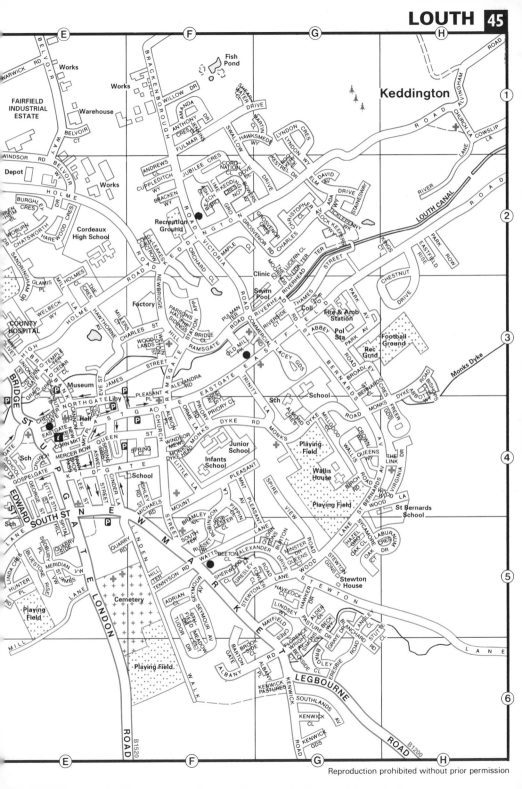

Keddington

FAIRFIELD INDUSTRIAL ESTATE

Cordeaux High School

COUNTY HOSPITAL

Recreation Ground

LOUTH CANAL

Monks Dyke

Football Ground

Fire & Amb Station

Swim Pool

Clinic

Museum

Junior School

Infants School

Wallis House

St Bernards School

Playing Field

Cemetery

Playing Field

LEGBOURNE

KENWICK PASTURES

Stewton House

Reproduction prohibited without prior permission

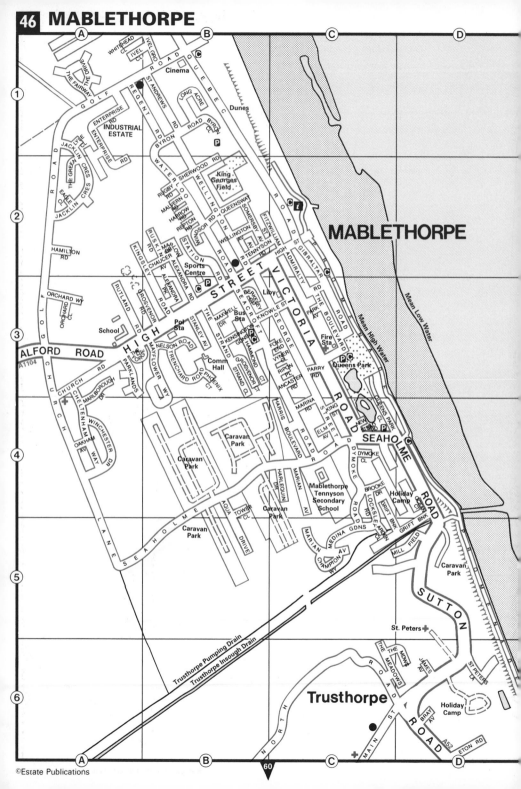

**MABLETHORPE**

Trusthorpe

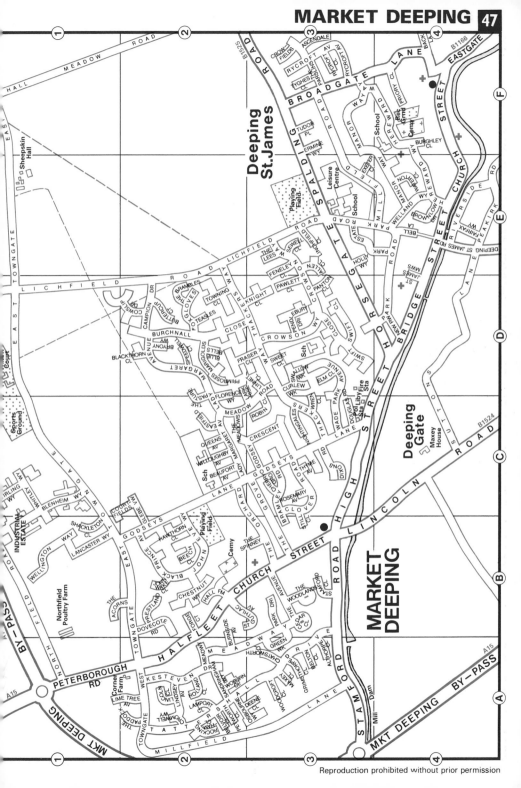

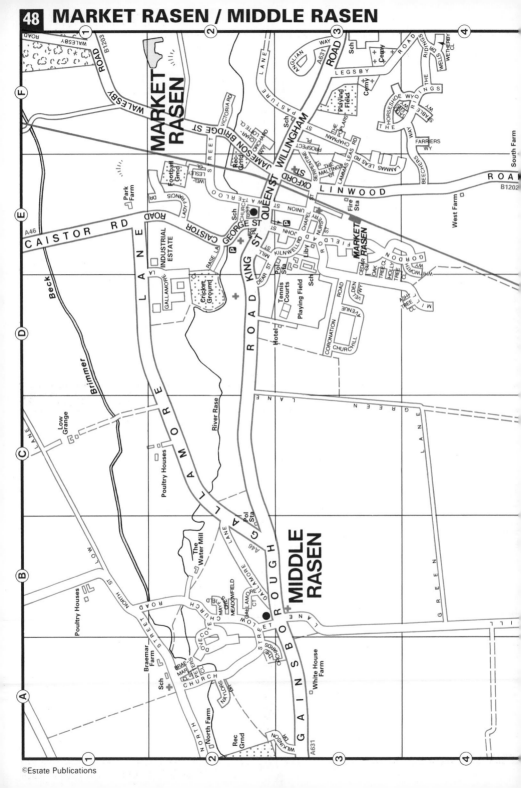

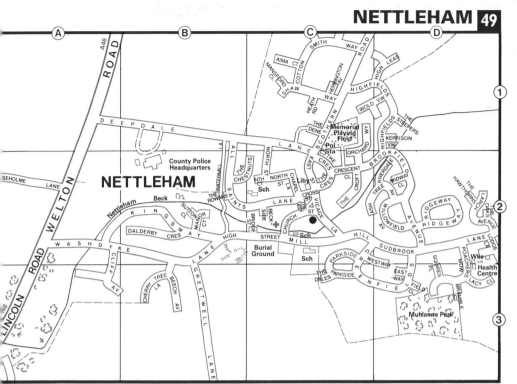

# RUSKINGTON

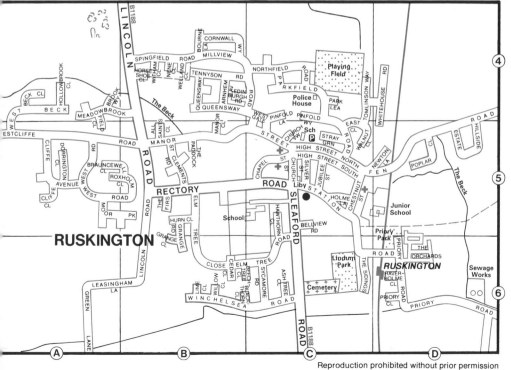

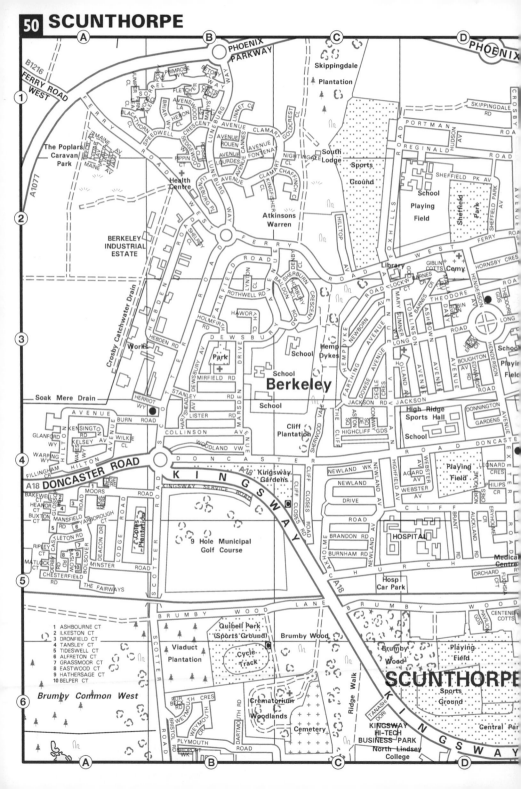

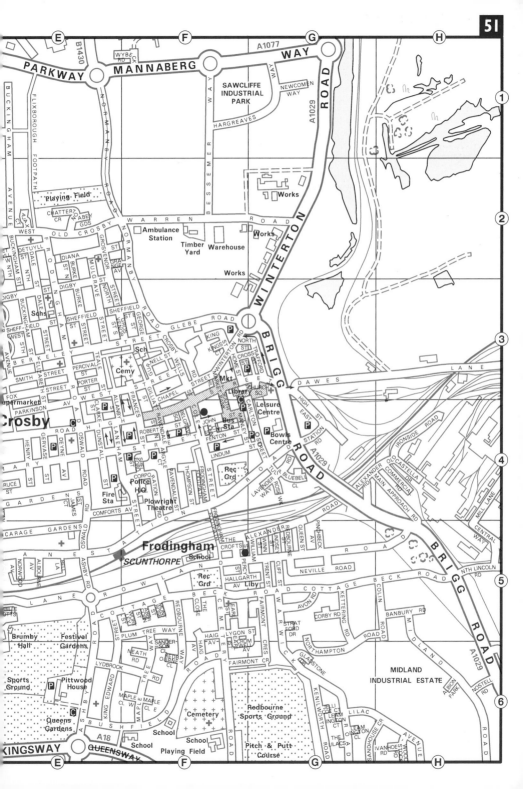

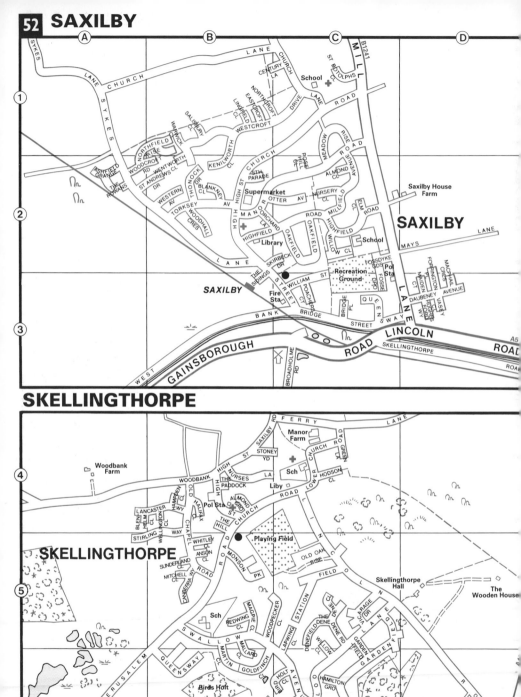

# SKELLINGTHORPE

SKELLINGTHORPE

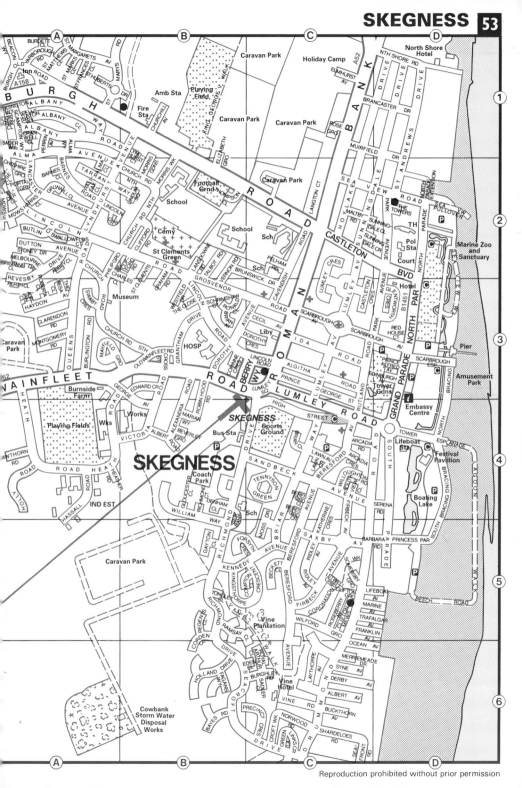

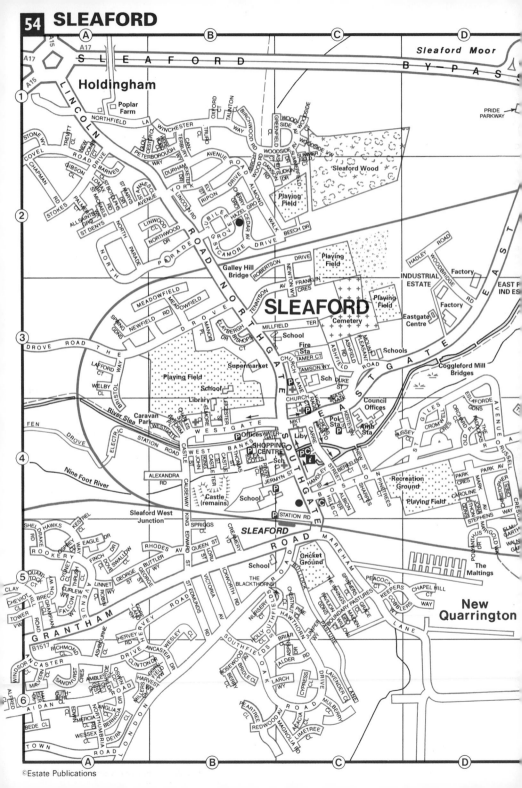

Evedon

ROAD

A153

SLEAFORD

Sewage Works

Sleaford North Junction

BONEMILL LANE

Bonemill Bridge

Royal Oak Bridge

Old River Slea

Slea Bridge

Old River Bridge

EVEDON ROAD

EVEDON

EVEDON

ROAD

Evedon Road Spinneys

The Grange

LANE

Sch

CHURCH

Kirkby la Thorpe

BY-PASS

UPLANDS

Boston Road Bridge

BOSTON

ROAD

SHELLEY

BURNS CRES

ELIOT CT

KIPLING DR

COLERIDGE GDNS

CRES

KEATS

RUSSELL

WAY

WAY

RUM

Sleaford South Junction

New Ballast Pit

Old Ballast Pit

ROAD

MOUNT

A17

MOUNT CL

MOUNT LANE

Bones Farm

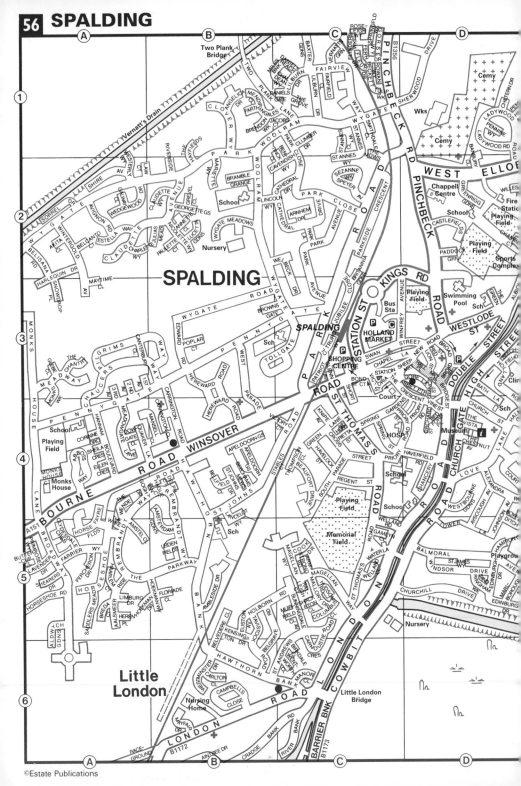

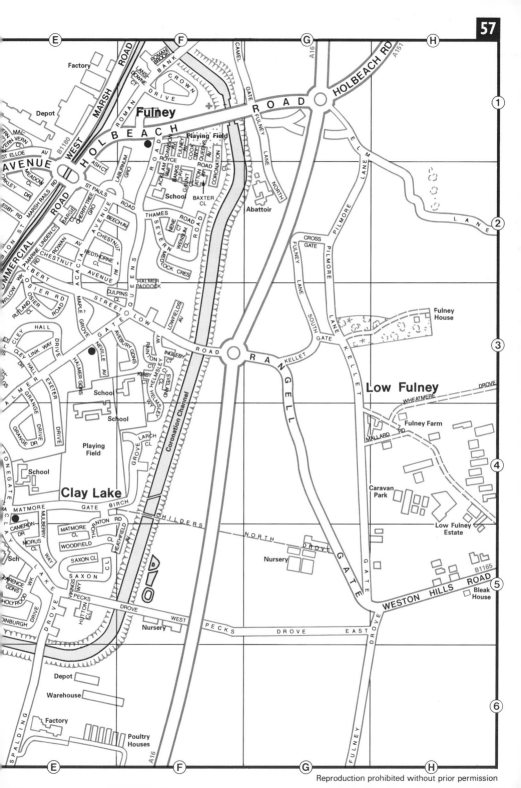

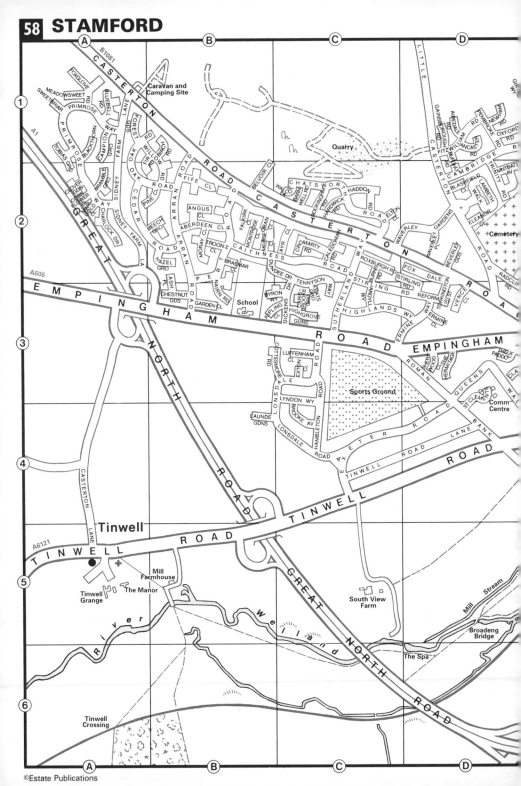

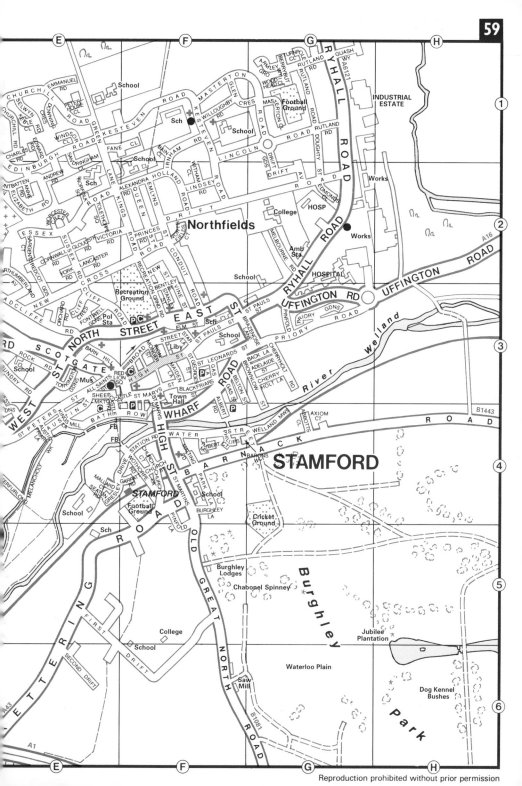

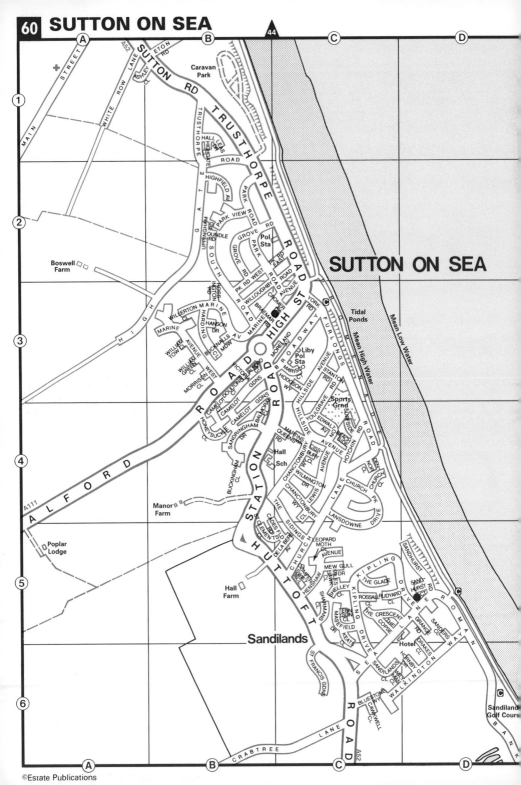

**SUTTON ON SEA**

Sandilands

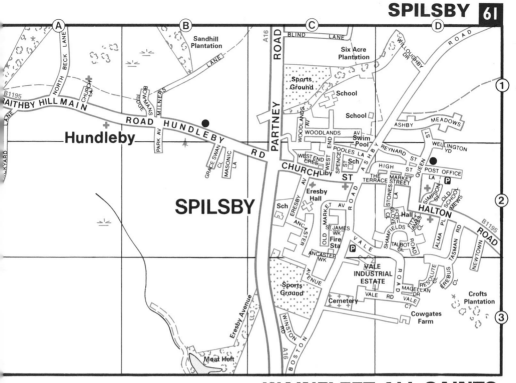

## SPILSBY

**Hundleby**

## WAINFLEET ALL SAINTS

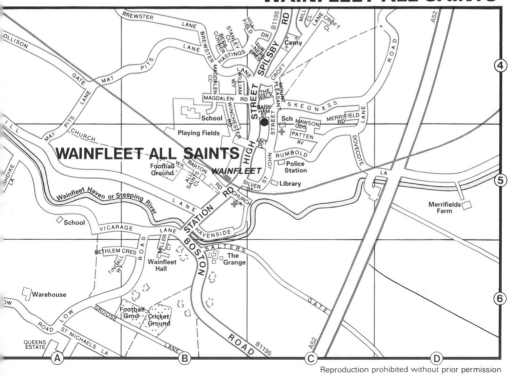

## WAINFLEET ALL SAINTS

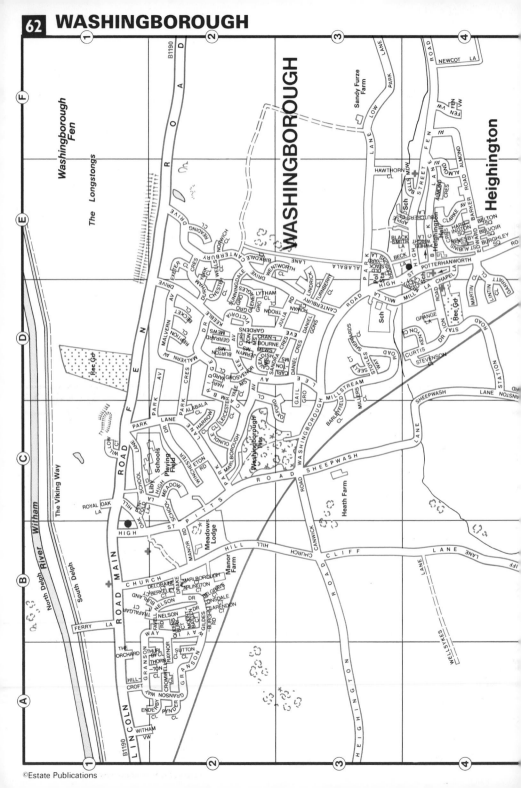

WASHINGBOROUGH

Heighington

Washingborough Fen

The Longstongs

Rec. Gd.

The Viking Way

River Witham

North Delph

South Delph

LINCOLN ROAD

B1190

ROAD MAIN

FERRY LA.

Sandy Furze Farm

NEWCOT LA.

PARK LANE LOW

FEN STREET

HAWTHORN CL.

BLACK SMITH LA.

POTTERHANWORTH

GRANGE

SHEEPWASH LANE

STATION ROAD

Heath Farm

HEIGHINGTON

CHURCH HILL

CLIFF

CANWICK

WELLSYKES

ROAD WASHINGBOROUGH

Washingborough Recs.

Playing Field

Schools

Lib.

ROYAL OAK LA.

HIGH

Meadows Lodge

Manor Farm

THE ORCHARD

HILL CROFT

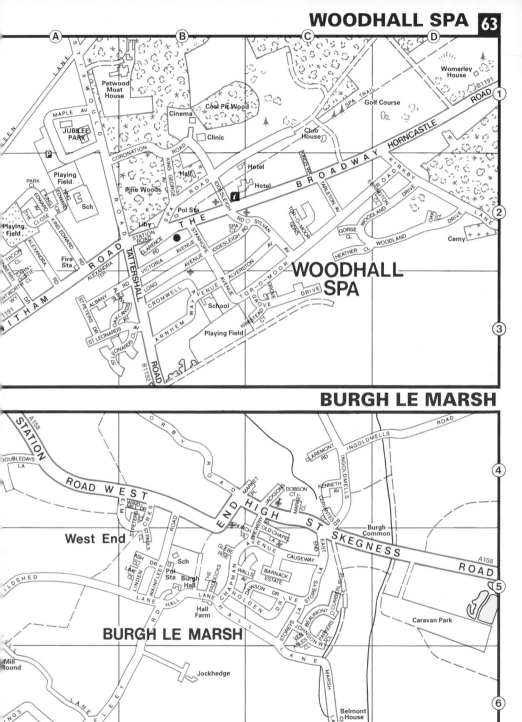

# BURGH LE MARSH

# A - Z INDEX TO STREETS
## with Postcodes

The Index includes some names for which there is insufficient space on the maps. These names are preceded by an * and are followed by the nearest adjoining thoroughfare.

Riverside Ind Est.
PE21 17 E1
Ingelow Av. PE21 14 C2
Ingram Rd. PE21 14 D2
Irby Pl. PE21 15 F4
Irby St. PE21 15 E3
Ivy Cres. PE21 14 D5
James St. PE21 15 E4
John Adams Way. PE21 15 F4
Joy Paine Clo. PE21 14 C2
Jubilee Av. PE21 15 E2
Judge Clo. PE21 16 B5
Kenleigh Dri. PE21 16 B4
King St. PE21 15 E5
Kings Av. PE21 14 A6
Kings Cres. PE21 16 A6
Kingsway. PE21 15 H5
Kitwood Clo. PE21 15 H5
Kitwood Rd. PE21 15 H5
Kyme Rd. PE21 14 D2
Ladds Clo. PE21 16 A5
Lambs Row. PE21 15 E3
Langrick Rd. PE21 14 C3
Larkspur Croft. PE21 14 C2
Laughton Rd. PE21 14 D3
Laval Pl. PE21 15 G4
Lawrence La. PE21 15 F4
Lealand Way. PE21 17 E1
Leverett Rd. PE21 15 H4
Levers Clo. PE21 16 D4
Lime Gro. PE21 16 A6
Lincoln La. PE21 15 E4
Linden Way. PE21 15 G1
*Lindis Ct,
Liquorpond St. PE21 15 F5
Lindis Rd. PE21 15 H3
Linley Clo. PE21 17 C1
Liquorpond St. PE21 15 E4
Locksley Clo. PE21 15 E2
Locomotive St. PE21 15 E5
London Rd,
Boston. PE21 15 F6
London Rd,
Wyberton. PE21 17 A4
Longhurst Gdns. PE21 14 D2
Low Rd. PE21 17 D4
Lyn Ellis Clo. PE21 16 A4
Main Ridge East. PE21 15 G4
Main Ridge West. PE21 15 F4
Manor Gdns. PE21 15 G4
Maple Rd. PE21 16 A6
Margaret Dri. PE21 15 H3
Marian Rd. PE21 15 E1
Market Pl. PE21 15 F4
Marsh Av. PE21 17 D1
Marsh La. PE21 17 D1
Mastins Ct. PE21 15 F3
Matthew Flinders Way.
PE21 14 D6
Maud St. PE21 15 G3
Mayfair Gdns. PE21 15 H2
Mayflower Rd. PE21 16 A5
Medforth La. PE21 15 E1
Medlam Rd. PE21 14 C5
Meridian Clo. PE21 16 B4
Meridian Rd. PE21 16 A4
Middle Drove. PE21 14 A2
Middlecot Clo. PE21 17 D1
Mill La. PE21 15 E4
Mill Lodge. PE21 15 G3
Mill Rd. PE21 15 H5
Mitre La. PE21 15 F3
Monteith Cres. PE21 15 H3
Mountains Pass. PE21 15 E4
Muster Roll La. PE21 15 G5
Nelson Way. PE21 15 F5
New Hammond Beck Rd.
PE21 14 A6
New St. PE21 15 F3
Norfolk Pl. PE21 15 E3
Norfolk St. PE21 15 E3
Norman Av. PE21 15 F3
North Forty Foot Bank.
PE21 14 A3
North St. PE21 15 F2
Nursery Rd. PE21 17 E1
Oak Cres. PE21 15 E2
Old Hammond Beck
Bank Rd. PE21 14 B6
Orchard St. PE21 14 D3
Oxford St. PE21 15 F5
Paddock Gro. PE21 15 F4
Park Gate. PE21 15 F3
Park La. PE21 15 E3
Park Rd. PE21 15 E6
Parsons Dri. PE21 15 E1

Parthian Av. PE21 17 B4
Peck Av. PE21 14 D5
Pen St. PE21 15 F3
Petticoat La. PE21 15 F4
Pettitt Way. PE21 16 A5
Pilgrim Rd. PE21 15 F4
Plover Clo. PE21 17 F2
Poplar Clo. PE21 14 D6
Porcher Way. PE21 14 D2
Portland St. PE21 15 E4
Princess Anne Rd. PE21 15 H3
Princess St. PE21 14 D4
Priory Rd. PE21 16 C4
Pulvertoft La. PE21 15 F5
Pump Sq. PE21 15 F4
Punchbowl La. PE21 14 A1
Puritan Way. PE21 14 D2
Quaker La. PE21 15 F4
Queen St. PE21 15 E4
Queens Rd. PE21 15 G3
Ralphs La. PE21 17 A4
Ransom Pl. PE21 15 E6
Raybrook Clo. PE21 15 E2
Reams Clo. PE21 16 B4
Rectory Rd. PE21 15 G5
Red Lion St. PE21 15 F3
Redcap La. PE21 15 E1
Regal Centre. PE21 15 F4
Revesby Av. PE21 14 D4
Revesby Clo. PE21 14 D4
Richmond Clo. PE21 15 G3
Rider Gdns. PE21 16 A6
River Way. PE21 15 H6
*Riverside Lodge,
South Sq. PE21 15 F4
Robin Hoods Walk.
PE21 15 E2
Rochford Cres. PE21 15 G3
Rochford Tower La.
PE21 16 B2
Rose Pl. PE21 15 G5
Rosebery Av. PE21 14 C4
Rosegarth St. PE21 15 E4
Rowan Way. PE21 15 G1
Rowdyke Rd. PE21 17 F4
Rowley Rd. PE21 15 F4
Ryton Rd. PE21 14 C5
St Anns La. PE21 15 F5
St Georges Rd. PE21 15 E4
St Johns Rd. PE21 15 F5
St Leodegars Clo. PE21 17 B4
St Leonard Clo. PE21 15 G2
St Marks Ter. PE21 15 F3
St Nicholas Clo. PE21 15 G5
St Nicholas Rd. PE21 15 F4
St Thomas Ct. PE21 17 D1
St Thomas Dri. PE21 17 D1
Saddlers Way. PE21 16 A6
*Sam Newsom Centre,
South Sq. PE21 15 F4
Sandringham Gdns.
PE21 16 A3
Saundergate La. PE21 17 B3
Saundergate La. East.
PE21 17 C4
Saundergate Pk. PE21 17 C4
Shaw Rd. PE21 14 C2
Sheriff Way. PE21 15 E1
Sherwood Av. PE21 15 E2
Shodfriars La. PE21 15 F4
Shortfield La. PE21 16 B1
Sibsey La. PE21 15 E1
Silt Pit La. PE21 17 F4
Silver St. PE21 15 F3
Sinclair Clo. PE21 15 E1
Sir Isaac Newton Dri.
PE21 17 D2
Skirbeck Rd. PE21 15 F5
Sleaford Rd. PE21 14 D3
Slippery Gowt La. PE21 17 E3
Smalley Rd. PE21 16 B5
Solhem Av. PE21 17 B4
Solway Av. PE21 17 C2
Somersby Grn. PE21 15 H2
Somersby Way. PE21 15 H2
South End. PE21 15 F5
South Par. PE21 14 C5
South Sq. PE21 15 F4
South St. PE21 15 F4
South Ter. PE21 15 F5
Spalding Rd. PE21 15 E5
Spalding Rd. PE21 17 B4
*Spain Ct,
Spain La. PE21 15 F4
Spain La. PE21 15 F4
Spain Pl. PE21 15 F4

Spayne Rd. PE21 15 F4
Spice Av. PE21 17 B3
Spilsby Rd. PE21 15 G3
Stafford St. PE21 15 E3
Stanbow La. PE21 15 F4
Standish Gro. PE21 15 G2
Stanhope Gdns. PE21 16 A4
Staniland Rd. PE21 14 D5
Station App. PE21 15 E4
Station St. PE21 15 E4
Stells La. PE21 15 F5
Stephenson Clo. PE21 17 D2
Still La. PE21 15 F4
Strait Bargate. PE21 15 F3
Sunningdale Dri. PE21 14 D3
Sussex Av. PE21 14 C4
Swineshead Rd. PE21 14 A6
Sydney St. PE21 14 D4
*Tattershall Ct,
Tattershall Rd. PE21 15 E3
Tattershall Rd. PE21 14 D1
Taverner Rd. PE21 14 D2
Tawney St. PE21 15 F3
Taylor Clo. PE21 16 B5
Tenens Way. PE21 17 E1
Tennyson Clo. PE21 15 E5
The Chase. PE21 16 A6
The Courtyard. PE21 15 G5
The Graylings. PE21 14 C2
The Orchard. PE21 17 B4
The Vineyards. PE21 15 E3
Thornton Av. PE21 14 D5
Thorold St. PE21 15 F3
Threadneedle St. PE21 15 F3
Tilney Av. PE21 14 D2
Tollfield Rd. PE21 15 H2
Tooley St. PE21 15 G5
Toot La. PE21 16 B5
Towell Clo. PE21 15 H6
Tower Rd. PE21 15 G3
Tower St. PE21 15 E4
Trafalgar Pl. PE21 15 E4
Trinity St. PE21 15 E4
Tudor Dri. PE21 15 E1
Tunnard St. PE21 15 F3
Tytton Clo. PE21 17 B2
Tytton Lane East. PE21 17 B2
Tytton Lane West. PE21 17 A2
Union Pl. PE21 15 E3
Union St. PE21 15 F3
Valentine Clo. PE21 15 G4
Vauxhall Rd. PE21 15 G4
Victoria Pl. PE21 15 F3
Vine Cres. PE21 17 B3
Wainfleet Rd. PE21 15 H1
Walden Gdns. PE21 14 D4
Ward Cres. PE21 16 C4
Washdyke La. PE21 14 B1
Welland Rd. PE21 14 B5
Wellington Rd. PE21 15 F4
West End Rd. PE21 17 A2
West St. PE21 15 E4
Westbridge Rd. PE21 14 A6
Westfield Av. PE21 14 D4
Wheeler Clo. PE21 15 G5
White House La. PE21 16 A5
Whitehorse La. PE21 15 F5
Whiting Sq. PE21 15 H1
Whittle Clo. PE21 17 D2
Wide Bargate. PE21 15 F3
Willoughby Rd. PE21 15 F1
Windsor Cres. PE21 15 G4
Windsor Ter. PE21 15 G4
Wing Dri. PE21 16 A5
Winslow Rd. PE21 15 F4
Winston Gdns. PE21 15 G2
Winter Way. PE21 17 B4
Witham Bank East.
PE21 15 E3
Witham Bank West.
PE21 15 E3
Witham Ct. PE21 15 E3
Witham Gdns. PE21 15 E3
Witham Grn. PE21 15 E3
Witham Pl. PE21 15 E3
Witham Town. PE21 15 E2
Woad Farm Rd. PE21 15 H1
Woodhall Rd. PE21 14 D3
Woodside. PE21 15 E4
Woodthorpe Av. PE21 16 A4
Woodville Gdns East.
PE21 14 D6
Woodville Gdns West.
PE21 14 D5
Woodville Rd. PE21 14 D4

Wormgate. PE21 15 F3
Wortleys La. PE21 14 A6
Wybert Cres. PE21 17 B3
Wybert La. PE21 17 E3
Wyberton Low Rd.
PE21 17 D1
Wyberton West Rd.
PE21 14 D6
Yarborough Rd. PE21 17 C2
Yew Tree Gro. PE21 16 A6
York St. PE21 15 G4
Zara Clo. PE21 15 H3

# BOURNE

Abbey Rd. PE10 18 C4
Abbots Clo. PE10 18 D5
Akeman Clo. PE10 18 B3
Alexandra Ter. PE10 18 C4
Ancaster Rd. PE10 18 D3
Arakan Way. PE10 18 D1
Arnhem Way. PE10 18 D2
Ash Gro. PE10 18 B2
Austerby. PE10 18 C4
Austerby Clo. PE10 18 C4
Aveland Clo. PE10 18 B3
Baldwin Gro. PE10 18 C3
Barkston Clo. PE10 18 D2
Beaufort Dri. PE10 18 B1
Bedehouse Bank. PE10 18 C4
Beech Av. PE10 18 A4
Berkeley Dri. PE10 18 B1
Betjeman Clo. PE10 18 C5
Bishops Clo. PE10 18 D5
Blackthorn Way. PE10 18 D3
Bourne Rd. PE10 18 D6
Brackley Clo. PE10 18 C1
Bramley Clo. PE10 18 B2
Briar Wk. PE10 18 C1
Broadlands Av. PE10 18 B2
Broadway Clo. PE10 18 B2
Bryony Gdns. PE10 18 C1
Burghley Ct. PE10 18 B3
Burghley St. PE10 18 B3
Burmoor Clo. PE10 18 D5
Carholme Clo. PE10 18 B2
Cecil Clo. PE10 18 A4
Cedar Dri. PE10 18 A2
Centurion Clo. PE10 18 D5
Charles Clo. PE10 18 C2
Cherry Holt Rd. PE10 18 D4
Cheriton Pk. PE10 18 C1
Chestnut Way. PE10 18 A4
Christophers La. PE10 18 B2
Church La. PE10 18 C4
Church View. PE10 18 C4
Churchill Av. PE10 18 A4
Coggles Causeway.
PE10 18 C4
Coleridge Dri. PE10 18 C5
Dere Clo. PE10 18 B3
Dorchester Av. PE10 18 D5
Drummond Rd. PE10 18 C4
East Gate. PE10 18 C4
Edinburgh Cres. PE10 18 C2
Edwin Gdns. PE10 18 A3
Elder Clo. PE10 18 B2
Elm Ter. PE10 18 C2
Ermine Clo. PE10 18 C4
Essex Way. PE10 18 C4
Exeter Clo. PE10 18 B3
Exeter Ct. PE10 18 B3
Exeter Gdns. PE10 18 B3
Exeter St. PE10 18 B3
Fir Av. PE10 18 A4
Forest Av. PE10 18 A3
Foxley Clo. PE10 18 B1
Galletly Clo. PE10 18 C2
George St. PE10 18 C3
Gladstone St. PE10 18 B2
Godiva Cres. PE10 18 A3
Godwin Clo. PE10 18 B2
Graham Hill Way. PE10 18 D4
*Granby Ct,
Manning Rd. PE10 18 C3
Grosvenor Av. PE10 18 D5
Hamilton Clo. PE10 18 D4
Harrington St. PE10 18 B2
Harvey Clo. PE10 18 A4
Hawthorn Rd. PE10 18 B2
Hazelwood Dri. PE10 18 A2
Heathcote Dri. PE10 18 D5
Hereward Bungalows.
PE10 18 A3

Hereward St. PE10 18 C3
Holland Clo. PE10 18 B3
Holly Dri. PE10 18 B2
Home Clo. PE10 18 B2
Jasmine Clo. PE10 18 A2
Kesteven Way. PE10 18 B3
Kingsley Av. PE10 18 A3
Kingsway. PE10 18 C2
Kohima Clo. PE10 18 D1
Laburnum Clo. PE10 18 B2
Larch Clo. PE10 18 B2
Lavender Way. PE10 18 A2
Leofric Av. PE10 18 A3
Lilac Clo. PE10 18 A2
Linden Rise. PE10 18 C1
Lodge Rd. PE10 18 B2
Lonsdale Gro. PE10 18 D2
Lyndsey Clo. PE10 18 B3
Mandalay Dri. PE10 18 D1
Manning Rd. PE10 18 C3
Manor Ct. PE10 18 B3
Manor La. PE10 18 C4
Maple Gdns. PE10 18 C3
Market Pl. PE10 18 C4
Meadow Clo. PE10 18 C3
Meadowgate. PE10 18 C3
Mercia Gdns. PE10 18 A3
Midleton Gdns. PE10 18 B2
Mill Drove. PE10 18 C4
Mountbatten Way. PE10 18 D1
Norman Mews. PE10 18 C3
North Rd. PE10 18 C3
North St. PE10 18 C3
Northfields. PE10 18 C2
Nowells La. PE10 18 C3
Oak Cres. PE10 18 A2
Oosterbeek Clo. PE10 18 D2
Orchard Clo. PE10 18 B2
Ostler Dri. PE10 18 A4
Pegasus Gro. PE10 18 D2
Pinewood Clo. PE10 18 A3
Pinfold Rd. PE10 18 D3
Poplar Cres. PE10 18 A3
Potters Clo. PE10 18 D4
Princes Ct. PE10 18 C3
Queens Rd. PE10 18 C3
Rangoon Way. PE10 18 D2
Recreation Rd. PE10 18 C3
Richardson Clo. PE10 18 C2
Rochester Ct. PE10 18 B1
Roman Bank. PE10 18 D5
Rowan Way. PE10 18 A2
St Gilberts Rd. PE10 18 B3
St Pauls Gdns. PE10 18 C4
St Peters Rd. PE10 18 B4
Saxon Way. PE10 18 A3
Sharpes Clo. PE10 18 C4
South Rd. PE10 18 C4
South St. PE10 18 C4
Southfields. PE10 18 C5
Spalding Rd. PE10 18 D4
Stanley St. PE10 18 B2
Stanton Clo. PE10 18 D3
Station App. PE10 18 C4
Stephenson Way. PE10 18 C1
Stone Clo. PE10 18 B2
Stretham Way. PE10 18 D4
Sycamore Clo. PE10 18 A3
Tannery Clo. PE10 18 D4
Tennyson Dri. PE10 18 C5
The Arena. PE10 18 B2
The Brambles. PE10 18 C1
*The Burghley Centre,
Market Pl. PE10 18 C3
The Retreat. PE10 18 B2
The Spindles. PE10 18 C1
Thurstan Clo. PE10 18 A3
Tin La. PE10 18 A3
Torfrida Dri. PE10 18 A3
Tunnel Bank. PE10 18 D5
Victor Way. PE10 18 D4
Victoria Pl. PE10 18 B2
Viking Clo. PE10 18 B2
Wakes Clo. PE10 18 D4
Waterside Clo. PE10 18 B2
Watling Clo. PE10 18 B3
Wendover Mews. PE10 18 D1
West Rd. PE10 18 A4
West St. PE10 18 A4
Westbourne Pk. PE10 18 A3
Westminster La. PE10 18 A3
Weswood Dri. PE10 18 A4
Wetherby Clo. PE10 18 B1
Wherrys La. PE10 18 B3
Willoughby Rd. PE10 18 D4
Willow Dri. PE10 18 B2

Wisteria Way. PE10   18 A2
Wingate Way. PE10   18 D1
Wood View. PE10   18 B3
Woodland Av. PE10   18 A3
Wordsworth Gro. PE10   18 C5
Yew Tree Clo. PE10   18 B2

## BRACEBRIDGE HEATH

Akeman Dri. LN4   12 C6
Alvis Clo. LN4   12 B6
Bath Rd. LN4   12 C5
Beech Clo. LN4   12 B6
Bentley Dri. LN4   12 B5
Bloxham La. LN4   12 D6
Bluebell Ct. LN4   12 C6
Bramble Ct. LN4   12 C6
Broadway. LN4   12 B5
Caistor Dri. LN4   12 B5
Canterbury Rd. LN4   12 C4
Canwick Av. LN4   12 B5
Car Dyke Way. LN4   12 C6
Carlisle Way. LN4   12 C4
Chichester Rd. LN4   12 C4
Churchill Av. LN4   12 B4
Clover Rd. LN4   12 B4
Cross O'Cliff Ct. LN4   12 B4
Davys La. LN4   12 B5
Dorothy Av. LN4   12 B5
Durham Clo. LN4   12 C4
East Av. LN4   12 B5
Ely Clo. LN4   12 C4
Fernleigh Av. LN4   12 C6
Fosse Ct. LN4   12 C6
Gloucester Clo. LN4   12 C4
Godber Dri. LN4   12 C6
Grange Rd. LN4   12 B6
Grantham Rd. LN4   12 B4
Hawthorn Clo. LN4   12 C6
Heath Rd. LN4   12 B6
Hillman Clo. LN4   12 B4
Home Clo. LN4   12 B4
Ickneld Clo. LN4   12 B6
Jensen Dri. LN4   12 B6
Johnson Dri. LN4   12 B5
Kennedy Rd. LN4   12 B5
King Dri. LN4   12 C6
Lagonda Clo. LN4   12 B6
Lancia Cres. LN4   12 B6
Lichfield Rd. LN4   12 C4
London Rd. LN4   12 B4
Main Av. LN4   12 B5
Maple Clo. LN4   12 C6
Mareham Clo. LN4   12 C6
Meadow Way. LN4   12 C6
Minster Clo. LN4   12 B4
Mount Rd. LN4   12 B5
Norfolk Cres. LN4   12 B4
Norwich Dri. LN4   12 C4
Oakdene Av. LN4   12 C6
Paddock Clo. LN4   12 B6
Park La. LN4   12 B4
Parkview Ct. LN4   12 B5
Peddars Ct. LN4   12 C6
Quintin Clo. LN4   12 B4
Redhall Dri. LN4   12 B4
Redhall La. LN4   12 B4
Renault Dri. LN4   12 B6
Ridgeway. LN4   12 C5
Ridgeview Rd. LN4   12 A5
Riley Clo. LN4   12 B6
Ripon Clo. LN4   12 C4
Rochester Clo. LN4   12 C4
St Albans Clo. LN4   12 C4
St Johns Rd. LN4   12 B5
St Johns Sq. LN4   12 B5
Salters Clo. LN4   12 C6
Salisbury Dri. LN4   12 C4
Sewstern Clo. LN4   12 C6
Sleaford Rd. LN4   12 B4
Southwell Clo. LN4   12 C4
Stane Dri. LN4   12 C6
Stanley Cres. LN4   12 B4
Stewards Way. LN4   12 B4
Sycamore Gro. LN4   12 C5
The Close. LN4   12 C5
The Crescent. LN4   12 B5
The Link. LN4   12 B4
Tower Av. LN4   12 B6
Vauxhall Rd. LN4   12 B6
Wakefield Dri. LN4   12 C4
Wells Dri. LN4   12 C4

Western Av. LN4   12 B5
Westminster Dri. LN4   12 C4
Whitehall Cres. LN4   12 B4
Willow Ct. LN4   12 C6
Winchester Clo. LN4   12 B5
Worcester Rd. LN4   12 C5

## BRIGG

Albert St. DN20   19 E3
Almond Gro. DN20   19 C2
Ancholme Gdns. DN20   19 D3
Ancholme Way. DN20   19 C3
Anchors Way. DN20   19 B3
Ash Gro. DN20   19 D2
Atherton Way. DN20   19 C2
Atkinson Av. DN20   19 E1
Barnard Av. DN20   19 C2
Bigby High Rd. DN20   19 E3
Bigby Rd. DN20   19 E3
Bigby St. DN20   19 D3
Birch Av. DN20   19 C2
Bramble Way. DN20   19 C2
Brickyard La. DN20   19 F1
Bridge St. DN20   19 D3
Brook La. DN20   19 A4
Burgess Rd. DN20   19 F3
Carr La. DN20   19 A1
Cary La. DN20   19 D3
Chapel Way. DN20   19 F2
Cherry Tree Av. DN20   19 D2
Churchill Av. DN20   19 F2
Colton St. DN20   19 D3
Cross St. DN20   19 D3
Davy Cres. DN20   19 D1
Davy Cres. DN20   19 D1
Dixon Clo. DN20   19 D2
Dudley Rd. DN20   19 D3
East Par. DN20   19 E2
Eastfield Rd. DN20   19 E3
Elm Way. DN20   19 C2
Elwes St. DN20   19 D3
Engine St. DN20   19 C3
Europa Way. DN20   19 C2
Forrester St. DN20   19 C3
Foxglove Clo. DN20   19 C2
Garden St. DN20   19 D3
Glanford Rd. DN20   19 E3
Glebe Rd. DN20   19 D2
Grammar School Rd. DN20   19 D2
Hawthorne Av. DN20   19 D2
Hedgerow La. DN20   19 C2
Highfield Gro. DN20   19 E1
Holme Clo. DN20   19 D2
Horstead Av. DN20   19 E1

**INDUSTRIAL & RETAIL:**
Ancholme Business Pk. DN20   19 C2
James St. DN20   19 D3
Kennedy Clo. DN20   19 F3
Kettleby Vw. DN20   19 F2
Kiln La. DN20   19 C3
Kings Av. DN20   19 D2
Kingsway. DN20   19 D2
Magrath Ct. DN20   19 D2
Manley Gdns. DN20   19 F3
Maple Clo. DN20   19 D3
Market La. DN20   19 D3
Market Pl. DN20   19 D3
Mill Clo. DN20   19 B3
Mill La. DN20   19 C3
Millers Quay. DN20   19 B3
New St. DN20   19 E3
Nicolgate La. DN20   19 E2
Northern Av. DN20   19 E1
O'Hanlon Av. DN20   19 F3
Old Courts Rd. DN20   19 D3
Paradise Pl. DN20   19 D3
Pingley La. DN20   19 F3
Pingley Mdw. DN20   19 F3
Poplar Dri. DN20   19 E1
Poppyfield Way. DN20   19 C2
Preston Dri. DN20   19 D2
Princes St. DN20   19 E3
Queen St. DN20   19 D3
Redcombe La. DN20   19 C2
Ridge Vw. DN20   19 F2
River Mdw. DN20   19 B4
Riverside. DN20   19 B3
St Clares Wk. DN20   19 D3
St Helens Rd. DN20   19 E3
St James St. DN20   19 F3
Scawby Rd. DN20   19 A4

Scunthorpe Rd. DN20   19 A3
Silversides La. DN20   19 B4
South View Av. DN20   19 E1
Springbank. DN20   19 D1
Springfield Rise. DN20   19 F2
Springfield Rd. DN20   19 F3
*Springs Par,
   Springs Way. SN20   19 D3
Springs Way. DN20   19 D3
Station Rd. DN20   19 D3
Sunningdale Av. DN20   19 D1
Teal Clo. DN20   19 B3
The Bottlings. DN20   19 D3
The Copse. DN20   19 F3
The Moorings. DN20   19 B3
The Narrow Boats.
  DN20   19 B3
Waters Edge. DN20   19 B3
Wellbeck Clo. DN20   19 F2
Wesley Rd. DN20   19 D2
West Sq. DN20   19 E2
West Ter. DN20   19 C3
Western Av. DN20   19 D1
Western Dri. DN20   19 E1
Westrum La. DN20   19 E4
Willowbrook Dri. DN20   19 F3
Winston Way. DN20   19 F2
Wold Vw. DN20   19 F2
Woodbine Av. DN20   19 F2
Wrawby Rd. DN20   19 E3
Wrawby St. DN20   19 D3
Yarborough Rd. DN20   19 F3
York Rd. DN20   19 F2

## BURGH LE MARSH

Ash Clo. PE24   63 B5
Barnack Est. PE24   63 C5
Beaumont Clo. PE24   63 C5
Billgate La. PE24   63 C6
Brewery St. PE24   63 B5
Causeway. PE24   63 C5
Cervantes Ct. PE24   63 C4
Chapman Av. PE24   63 B5
Church Hill. PE24   63 C5
Claremont Rd. PE24   63 C4
Cumberlidge Clo. PE24   63 C5
Dawson Dri. PE24   63 C5
Dobson St. PE24   63 C4
Doubledays La. PE24   63 A4
East End. PE24   63 C5
Elm Cres. PE24   63 B4
Glebe Rise. PE24   63 B5
Hall La. PE24   63 B5
High La. PE24   63 A6
High St. PE24   63 C4
Holden Dri. PE24   63 B5
Ingoldmells Rd. PE24   63 C4
Ings La. PE24   63 A6
Jacksons La. PE24   63 C4
Jock Hedge. PE24   63 C6
Johnson Way. PE24   63 C5
Kenneth Av. PE24   63 C4
Lime Clo. PE24   63 B5
Linden Dri. PE24   63 B5
Low La. PE24   63 A6
Market Clo. PE24   63 C4
Market Pl. PE24   63 C4
Marsh La. PE24   63 C6
Mill La. PE24   63 A5
Old Chapel La. PE24   63 C5
Orby Rd. PE24   63 B4
Parkers Clo. PE24   63 C5
St Pauls Clo. PE24   63 B5
St Peters Clo. PE24   63 B4
Skegness Rd. PE24   63 C5
Station Rd. PE24   63 A4
Storeys La. PE24   63 C5
The Paddocks. PE24   63 B5
Venables Rd. PE24   63 B5
Wainfleet Rd. PE24   63 B5
Walls Av. PE24   63 B5
West End. PE24   63 A4
Wildshed La. PE24   63 A5
Windmill Pl. PE24   63 B4

## CAISTOR

Ayscough Gro. LN7   20 B2
Bank La. LN7   20 C2
Bobs La. LN7   20 D2

Brigg Rd. LN7   20 B1
Burnetts Yd. LN7   20 D2
Caistor By-Pass. LN7   20 B2
Canada La. LN7   20 C1
Castle Hill. LN7   20 C2
Centurian Way. LN7   20 A2
Chapel St. LN7   20 C2
Cherry Holt. LN7   20 C2
Chichester Dri. LN7   20 C2
Church St. LN7   20 C2
Cromwell View. LN7   20 C2
Enterprise Rd. LN7   20 A2
Fountain St. LN7   20 C2
George Mews. LN7   20 D2
Grimsby Rd. LN7   20 D2
Hansard Cres. LN7   20 C2
Hersey Rd. LN7   20 B2
High St. LN7   20 C2
Horse Mkt. LN7   20 C2

**INDUSTRIAL ESTATE:**
North Kelsey Rd
  Ind Est. LN7   20 A2
Kelsway. LN7   20 B2
Keyworth Dri. LN7   20 C1
Knapton Ct. LN7   20 D1
Lincoln Rd. LN7   20 B3
Mallard Dri. LN7   20 B2
Mill La. LN7   20 D2
Millfields. LN7   20 B2
Moor La. LN7   20 A1
Navigation La. LN7   20 B2
Nettleton Rd. LN7   20 C3
Newbould Clo. LN7   20 B3
North Kelsey Rd. LN7   20 A1
North St. LN7   20 C2
Partridge Clo. LN7   20 B2
Pheasant Ct. LN7   20 C2
Plough Hill. LN7   20 C2
Plover Sq. LN7   20 B2
Rawlinson Av. LN7   20 C2
Risedale. LN7   20 C3
Saxon Way. LN7   20 B2
Saxonfields. LN7   20 B2
South Dale. LN7   20 C2
South St. LN7   20 D2
Spa Top. LN7   20 D1
Tennyson Clo. LN7   20 B3
*The George Ct,
  South St. LN7   20 D2
The Meadow. LN7   20 B2
The Ropewalk. LN7   20 D1
Varlow Rd. LN7   20 D2
Vicarage Clo. LN7   20 D2
Westwold Rd. LN7   20 C2
Whitegate Hill. LN7   20 D3
Windsor Dri. LN7   20 C2
Wold Vw. LN7   20 D2

## CHAPEL ST. LEONARDS

Acacia Av. PE24   21 C2
Ancaster Av. PE24   21 C2
Anderby Rd. PE24   21 C1
Andrew Av. PE24   21 C4
Beach Av. PE24   21 C3
Beatrice Way. PE24   21 C4
Brocks Clo. PE24   21 B4
Buckingham Dri. PE24   21 C2
Chapel Clo. PE24   21 C2
Chapel Farm Dri. PE24   21 B4
Church Farm Clo. PE24   21 B4
Church La. PE24   21 B4
Church Meadow Dri.
  PE24   21 B4
Connaught Dri. PE24   21 C3
Crown Av. PE24   21 C2
East View Clo. PE24   21 C4
Elizabeth Clo. PE24   21 B3
Elizabeth Ct. PE24   21 B3
Elizabeth Dri. PE24   21 B3
Elliott Way. PE24   21 C4
Fairburn Clo. PE24   21 C3
Fairfield Clo. PE24   21 C4
Gatram Rd. PE24   21 C5
Grassmere Av. PE24   21 D6
Jubilee Par. PE24   21 C3
Landseer Av. PE24   21 C2
Lindum Gro. PE24   21 C4
Marine Av. PE24   21 B3
Meadow Clo. PE24   21 B4
Palma Ct. PE24   21 B2
Parkside Av. PE24   21 C3

Parkside Dri. PE24   21 C3
Prince Av. PE24   21 B3
Promenade. PE24   21 D2
Regina Walk. PE24   21 C3
Rowan Ct. PE24   21 C3
St Leonards Dri. PE24   21 B3
Sandy La. PE24   21 D4
Sea Bank Rd. PE24   21 C2
Sea Rd. PE24   21 B3
Skegness Rd. PE24   21 B5
South Cres. PE24   21 C2
South Rd. PE24   21 C4
Sunningdale Clo. PE24   21 C4
Sunningdale Dri. PE24   21 C4
Swallow Clo. PE24   21 B3
The Green. PE24   21 D3
The Pullover. PE24   21 D4
Trunch La. PE24   21 B6
Tylers Clo. PE24   21 B3
Warwick Rd. PE24   21 C2
Waterside Way. PE24   21 C2
Well Vale Clo. PE24   21 C4
Well Vale Dri. PE24   21 C4
West View Cres. PE24   21 B4
Wigg La. PE24   21 B1
Wilton Av. PE24   21 C3
Workhouse La. PE24   21 A1

## CLEETHORPES

Acorn Ct. DN35   23 B7
Adams Rd. DN35   22 B3
Albert Rd. DN35   22 D4
Aldrich Rd. DN35   23 D6
Alexandra Rd. DN35   22 D3
Altyre Way. DN36   23 A8
Alvingham Av. DN35   23 D6
Ann Gro. DN35   23 B6
Applegarth Clo. DN35   23 B5
Arden Village. DN35   23 D8
Arundel Pl. DN35   23 C5
Ash Ct. DN35   23 B7
Ashby Rd. DN35   23 B6
Ashridge Dri. DN35   23 A5
Aspen Ct. DN35   23 C7
Balmoral Rd. DN35   23 A5
Barcroft St. DN35   22 A2
Bark St. DN35   22 D4
Barkhouse Clo. DN35   22 E4
Barkhouse La. DN35   22 D4
Barnett Pl. DN35   22 A2
Bassett Rd. DN35   23 E5
Beacon Av. DN35   22 B4
Beacon Ct. DN32   22 B4
Beaconthorpe Rd.
  DN35   22 C3
Beaufort Cres. DN35   23 B7
Beck Walk. DN35   23 C8
Beckside Clo. DN35   23 C8
Bedale Pl. DN35   23 C7
Bedford Rd. DN35   23 E8
Beech Way. DN35   23 B7
Beeley Rd. DN32   22 A4
Beesby Dri. DN35   23 D6
Belmont Clo. DN35   23 B6
Belvoir Park Wk. DN35   23 B7
Belvoir Rd. DN35   23 B7
Bennett Rd. DN35   22 B2
Bentley St. DN35   22 B4
Berkeley Rd. DN35   23 E8
Berners Rd. DN35   23 F8
Bestall Rd. DN32   22 B4
Billinghay Ct. DN35   23 D6
Bishopthorpe Rd. DN35   23 D6
Blakeney La. DN35   23 C8
Blenheim Pl. DN35   23 C5
Blundell Av. DN35   22 A2
Bolingbroke Rd. DN35   23 E6
Bowling La. DN35   22 C4
Bradford Av. DN35   23 D5
Braemar Rd. DN35   23 C6
Bramble Way. DN35   23 C8
Bramhall St. DN35   22 B2
Brampton Way. DN35   23 B6
Brereton Av. DN35   22 A2
Brian Av. DN35   23 A6
Brighton St. DN35   22 E4
Brooklands Av. DN35   23 E5
Brooklyn Dri. DN36   23 F8
Broughton Dri. DN35   23 B8
Buck Beck Way. DN35   23 B8
Bullfinch La. DN35   23 C8
Burley La. DN35   23 D6
Burnham Reach. DN35   23 D8

Bursar St. DN35 22 C4
Butterwick Clo. DN35 23 D6
Caenby Rd. DN35 23 D8
Cambridge St. DN35 22 D4
Campden Cres. DN35 22 B3
Carlton Clo. DN35 23 F8
Carlyle Clo. DN35 23 E8
Carr La. DN32 22 A3
Carrington Dri. DN36 23 F8
Cattistock Rd. DN35 23 C7
Cavendish Clo. DN35 23 E8
Cedar Clo. DN35 23 B7
Central Prom. DN35 22 D3
Chaffinch Dri. DN35 23 C8
Chapman Gro. DN35 22 D4
Chapman Rd. DN35 22 B2
Charles St. DN35 22 D4
Chatsworth Pl. DN35 23 A5
Chelsea Wk. DN35 23 E8
Cheltenham Way.
  DN35 23 D8
Cherry Dale. DN35 23 B6
Chester Pl. DN35 23 A5
Chichester Rd. DN35 23 D6
Church La. DN32 22 A4
Claremont Rd. DN32 22 B4
Claymore Clo. DN35 22 C4
Clee Cres. DN32 22 A4
Clee Ness Dri. DN36 23 E8
Clee Rd. DN32 22 A4
Clee Village. DN35 22 A4
Clixby Clo. DN35 23 E6
Clumber Pl. DN35 23 C5
College St. DN35 22 C3
Combe St. DN35 22 A2
Conyard Rd. DN35 22 C3
Coronation Rd. DN35 22 D4
Cosgrove St. DN35 22 D3
Cottesmore Rd. DN35 23 C7
Coulbeck Dri. DN35 23 B5
Craithie Rd. DN35 23 C5
Crampin Rd. DN35 23 A6
Cranbourne Clo. DN35 23 D8
Criding Rd. DN35 23 B5
Cromwell Rd. DN35 23 E5
Cross St. DN35 22 C3
Crow Hill Av. DN35 22 C4
Cumberland Rd. DN35 23 E8
Curzon Av. DN35 23 B5
Curzon Ct. DN35 23 E8
Cuttleby. DN35 22 D4
Cynthia Rd. DN32 22 A4
Daggett Rd. DN35 23 E6
Daubney St. DN35 22 A2
Davenport Dri. DN35 23 A5
Delamere St. DN35 23 D8
Denby Dri. DN35 23 A6
Dolphin St. DN35 22 D3
Douglas Rd. DN35 22 B2
Dudley Pl. DN35 23 B5
Durham Rd. DN35 23 A5
Edward St. DN35 22 C4
Elderberry Way. DN35 23 B7
Elliston St. DN35 22 A2
Elm Av. DN35 22 C4
Elm Rd. DN35 22 C4
Elwyn Pl. DN35 23 B7
Eskham Clo. DN35 23 D6
Fair View Av. DN35 22 C4
Fairfield Ct. DN35 23 E8
Fairways. DN35 23 E8
Fernie Pl. DN35 23 C7
Field House Rd. DN36 23 E8
Fillingham Cres. DN35 23 D6
Fisher Pl. DN35 22 B3
Fitzwilliam Mews.
  DN35 23 C7
Frankland Pl. DN35 22 B2
Frederick St. DN35 22 C3
Frobisher Av. DN35 22 A4
Fuller St. DN35 22 B2
Garbutt Pl. DN35 23 E5
Garnett St. DN35 22 B2
Gayton Rd. DN35 23 E6
George St. DN35 22 D4
Giles St. DN35 22 C4
Glebe Rd. DN35 22 D4
Goring Pl. DN35 22 B3
Grainsby Av. DN35 23 B6
Grant St. DN35 22 C3
Green Hill. DN35 23 B6
Greenfinch Dri. DN35 23 C8
Greethams La. DN32 22 A4
Grimsby Rd. DN35 22 A1
Grimsby Rd. DN36 23 B7
Grosvenor Ct. DN35 23 E8

Grove Cres. DN32 22 A3
Gunby Pl. DN35 23 C5
Haigh St. DN35 22 E4
Haile Rd. DN36 23 E8
Halton Pl. DN35 23 B6
Hamont Rd. DN32 22 A3
Hampton Ct. DN35 23 B5
Hampton St. DN35 23 D8
Hardys Rd. DN35 23 D5
Harewood Gro. DN35 23 D8
Harrington St. DN35 22 A1
Hart St. DN35 22 A2
Haverstoe Pl. DN35 23 A6
Hawthorne Av. DN35 22 B2
Hayling Mere. DN35 23 D8
Helene Gro. DN32 22 A3
Hewitts Av. DN36 23 A8
Hewitts Manor. DN35 23 B7
Hey St. DN35 23 D5
Heythorp Rd. DN35 23 C7
High St. DN35 22 D3
High Thorpe Cres.
  DN35 23 B6
Highcliff Rd. DN35 23 E4
Highgate. DN35 22 D4
Hilton Ct. DN35 23 F8
Hinkler St. DN35 22 C4
Hollingsworth Clo.
  DN35 23 B7
Holyoake Av. DN32 22 A4
Honeysuckle Clo. DN35 23 C8
Hope St. DN35 22 E4
Howlett Rd. DN35 23 E5
Humber St. DN35 22 D4
Humberston Rd. DN35 23 A5
Hurst Lea Dri. DN36 23 F8
Hutchinson Rd. DN35 22 C2
Imperial Av. DN35 22 A2
Ingram St. DN35 23 B7
Irby Ct. DN35 23 B6
Isaacs Hill. DN35 22 C3
Itterby Cres. DN35 23 A6
Kathleen Clo. DN35 22 B2
Kathleen Gro. DN32 22 A3
Kelham Rd. DN32 22 B4
Kenilworth Rd. DN35 23 B5
Kew Rd. DN35 22 C4
Kings Par. DN35 22 E4
Kings Rd. DN35 23 E5
Kingston Clo. DN35 23 E8
Kingsway. DN35 23 E4
Knoll St. DN35 22 D4
Kymer Pl. DN35 23 E5
Lady Frances Cres.
  DN35 22 A4
Lairgate Pl. DN35 35 D8
Lambourne Ct. DN35 23 D8
Langley Pl. DN35 23 E6
Lansdown Link. DN35 23 C6
Larch Way. DN35 23 B7
Lestrange St. DN35 22 A3
Lewis Rd. DN35 22 B2
Lincoln Rd. DN35 23 A5
Lindsey Rd. DN35 23 D5
Lindum Rd. DN35 23 D5
Links Rd. DN35 23 E6
Loveden Ct. DN35 23 E6
Lovett St. DN35 22 A2
Ludborough Way.
  DN35 23 D6
Ludlow Pl. DN35 23 C5
Lynton Rise. DN35 23 C6
Manchester St. DN35 22 B2
Manley Gdns. DN35 23 E6
Marigold Wk. DN35 23 C8
Market St. DN35 22 D3
Marlborough Way.
  DN35 23 D8
Marples Mws. DN35 22 E4
Marsh Chapel Clo.
  DN35 23 D6
Martyn Rd. DN35 22 B3
Mathews St. DN35 22 A2
May St. DN35 22 B2
Mayfair Ct. DN35 23 E8
Meadow Vw. DN35 23 D8
Middle Thorpe Rd.
  DN35 23 B6
Mill Garth. DN35 23 B7
Mill Hill Cres. DN35 22 C4
Mill Pl. DN35 22 C4
Mill Rd. DN35 22 C4
Miller Av. DN32 22 B3
Minshull Rd. DN35 23 D6
Mollison Av. DN35 22 D4

Montgomery Rd. DN35 22 B4
Morgan Way. DN35 22 C4
Neptune St. DN35 22 C2
Neville St. DN35 22 B2
New Rd. DN35 22 B3
Newlands Pk. DN36 23 F8
Newstead Rd. DN35 23 C5
Nicholson St. DN35 23 D5
Norfolk La. DN35 22 C3
Normandy Rd. DN35 22 B4
North Prom. DN35 22 C2
North Sea La. DN35 23 D8
North St. DN35 22 D4
Oak Way. DN35 23 B7
Oliver St. DN35 22 B2
Oole Rd. DN35 22 D4
Ormsby Clo. DN35 23 B6
Osbourne St. DN35 22 D3
Oslear Cres. DN35 22 C4
Oxford St. DN35 22 D4
Oyster Ct. DN35 22 E4
Park La. DN35 23 D8
Park View. DN35 22 A2
Parker St. DN35 22 D5
Parris Pl. DN35 22 B3
Pearson Rd. DN35 23 D6
Pelham Av. DN35 22 C3
Pelham Sq. DN35 22 C2
Pendreth Pl. DN35 22 B3
Penshurst Rd. DN35 23 B5
Phelps Pl. DN32 22 A4
Phelps St. DN35 22 A1
Philip Av. DN35 23 B5
Philip Gro. DN35 23 B6
Pine Ct. DN35 23 C8
Poplar Dri. DN36 23 F8
Poplar Gro. DN35 22 C3
Poplar Rd. DN35 22 C3
Primrose Way. DN35 23 C8
Princes Rd. DN35 22 C3
Prystie Pl. DN35 23 B7
Pytchley Wk. DN35 23 C7
Queen Mary Av. DN35 22 A2
Queens Par. DN35 23 D5
Quorn Mews. DN35 23 C7
Ravendale Rd. DN35 23 E6
Ravenhill Clo. DN35 23 B6
Redwood Dri. DN35 23 B7
Reston Ct. DN35 23 E6
Reynolds St. DN35 22 B3
Richmond Rd. DN35 23 C5
Riverside Dri. DN35 23 F8
Robson Rd. DN35 22 B3
Rochester Ct. DN35 23 E8
Rosemary Way. DN35 23 C8
Rowston St. DN35 22 E4
Rufford Rd. DN35 23 C5
Russell St. DN35 23 E8
St Heliers Av. DN35 22 C3
St Hughs Av. DN35 22 C4
St Marys Clo. DN32 22 A4
St Peters Av. DN35 22 C3
Sandringham Rd. DN35 23 B5
Saxby Gro. DN35 22 C3
Saxon Cres. DN35 22 C4
School Wk. DN35 23 A5
Scrivelsby Ct. DN35 23 E7
Sea Rd. DN35 22 D3
Sea View St. DN35 22 D4
Seacroft Rd. DN35 23 E5
Seaford Rd. DN35 23 E8
Segmere St. DN35 22 E4
Sherburn St. DN35 23 C5
Signhills Av. DN35 23 E5
Simons Pl. DN35 22 B3
Solomon St. DN35 23 B5
South St. DN35 22 D4
Stanhope Pl. DN35 22 A3
Station Rd. DN35 22 D3
Stevenson Pl. DN35 22 B4
Strubby Clo. DN35 23 E6
Suggitts Ct. DN35 22 B2
Suggitts La. DN35 22 B2
Suggitts Orchard. DN35 22 C2
Swaby Clo. DN35 23 B6
Taylors Av. DN35 23 B7
Tennyson Rd. DN35 22 C3
Terrington St. DN35 23 B5
The Gathering. DN35 22 C4
Thoresby Pl. DN35 23 C6
Thorganby Rd. DN35 23 E6
Thornton Cres. DN35 23 C5
Thruncoe Rd. DN35 23 D5
Tiverton St. DN35 22 A2
Trinity Rd. DN35 23 C5
Twyning Pl. DN35 22 B2

Unity Rd. DN32 22 A4
Violet Clo. DN35 23 C8
Waldorf Rd. DN35 23 E8
Walnut Cres. DN35 23 B7
Ward St. DN35 22 A2
Wardall St. DN35 22 B2
Warneford Rd. DN35 22 B2
Warwick Rd. DN35 23 B5
Weekes Rd. DN35 23 D6
Welbeck Rd. DN35 23 A5
Wells Cres. DN35 23 C7
Wendover Rise. DN35 23 C6
Wesley Cres. DN35 23 C6
West St. DN35 22 D4
Westbury Pk. DN35 23 E8
Westbury Rd. DN35 23 E8
Westfield Gro. DN35 22 B4
Westport Rd. DN35 23 E8
Weyford Rd. DN35 23 E8
Whitehall Country Cotts.
  DN35 23 E8
Whitehall Rd. DN35 23 E8
Whites Rd. DN35 23 D5
William St. DN35 22 D4
Wilson St. DN35 22 B2
Wilton Rd. DN36 23 B8
Windermere Cres.
  DN36 23 C8
Windsor Rd. DN35 23 A5
Winn Ct. DN35 22 C4
Wollaston Rd. DN35 22 C4
Woodland Wk. DN35 23 C8
Woodsley Av. DN35 23 C5
Yarra Rd. DN35 23 A5
York Pl. DN35 23 A5

## CONINGSBY/TATTERSHALL

Abbey Clo. LN4 24 C1
Allen Rd. LN4 24 F1
Ash Rd. LN4 24 E3
Baxter Clo. LN4 24 E3
Beech Clo. LN4 24 E3
Birch Clo. LN4 24 E3
Blacksmiths Cnr. LN4 24 B2
Blenheim Rd. LN4 24 E3
Brent Rd. LN4 24 A3
Butts La. LN4 24 C2
Canberra Clo. LN4 24 D3
Carrington Clo. LN4 24 E2
Castle La. LN4 24 D2
Castle View. LN4 24 A2
Cherrytree Way. LN4 24 E3
Chestnut Dri. LN4 24 E3
Coldham Rd. LN4 24 F1
Cooke Cres. LN4 24 E3
Croft La. LN4 24 A3
Cromwell Pl. LN4 24 B2
Curzon Est. LN4 24 B2
Dogdyke Rd. LN4 24 C4
East Dri. LN4 24 A3
Fairfield. LN4 24 D2
Farriers Way. LN4 24 A2
Finney Clo. LN4 24 E1
Fortescue Clo. LN4 24 A2
Gayle Rd. LN4 24 A3
Granary La. LN4 24 B2
Greenfield Rd. LN4 24 E2
Harness Dri. LN4 24 B2
Heathcote Rd. LN4 24 E1
High St,
  Coningsby. LN4 24 D2
High St,
  Tattershall. LN4 24 D2
Hoplands Clo. LN4 24 E2
Horseshoe Clo. LN4 24 B1
Hudson Dri. LN4 24 F1
Hunters La. LN4 24 C2
Ingham Ct. LN4 24 F1
Ingham Rd. LN4 24 F1
Kirby La. LN4 24 D1
Lancaster Dri. LN4 24 D3
Laythorpe Gdns. LN4 24 D2
Lewis Rd. LN4 24 E3
Lodge Rd. LN4 24 A3
Manor La. LN4 24 A3
Market Pl. LN4 24 D2
Marmion Rd. LN4 24 E1
Marsh La. LN4 24 A2
Masons La. LN4 24 D2
Mill Farm Est. LN4 24 B1
Milson Clo. LN4 24 D2
Mitchell Rd. LN4 24 F1

North La. LN4 24 A3
Old Boston Rd. LN4 24 D2
Old Smithy Ct. LN4 24 D2
Orchard Way. LN4 24 D3
Overton Rd. LN4 24 E3
Park La. LN4 24 D2
Pringle Clo. LN4 24 E1
Providence Pl. LN4 24 E1
Read Way. LN4 24 E1
School La. LN4 24 D2
Shannon Rd. LN4 24 E3
Sherwood Rd. LN4 24 E3
Silver St. LN4 24 D2
Sleaford Rd. LN4 24 A3
Stenner Rd. LN4 24 F1
Teal Rd. LN4 24 A3
The Park. LN4 24 E2
Thorpe Pl. LN4 24 C1
Thorpe Rd. LN4 24 C2
Tomlinson Clo. LN4 24 B2
Tumby Rd. LN4 24 E1
Washington Clo. LN4 24 D3
Wesselow Rd. LN4 24 F1
West Dri. LN4 24 A3
Wharfe La. LN4 24 D1
Willow Dri. LN4 24 E2
Willows Ct. LN4 24 B2

## CROWLAND

Abbey Mews. PE6 20 C5
Abbey Walk. PE6 20 C5
Abbots Dri. PE6 20 B5
Albion St. PE6 20 B5
Alderlands Clo. PE6 20 B6
Ambury Gdns. PE6 20 C4
Barbers Drove. PE6 20 C6
Becclesm Dri. PE6 20 C6
Broadway. PE6 20 B5
Chapel St. PE6 20 C6
Church La. PE6 20 C4
Cloot Drove. PE6 20 C4
Cluttons Clo. PE6 20 C5
Coronation Av. PE6 20 B6
Crawford Gdns. PE6 20 B6
Crease Drove. PE6 20 C6
Croyland Way. PE6 20 C5
East St. PE6 20 C4
Eastlands. PE6 20 C4
First Drove. PE6 20 B4
Foreman Way. PE6 20 D4
Girdlestone Walk. PE6 20 C4
Glebe Gdns. PE6 20 B6
Godiva Clo. PE6 20 D5
Gravel Causeway. PE6 20 A4
Hall St. PE6 20 C5
Harrington Way. PE6 20 C6
Hereward Way. PE6 20 C5
High Wash Drove. PE6 20 A4
Horseshoe Yd. PE6 20 B5
Jareys Clo. PE6 20 B5
Jubilee Way. PE6 20 C4
Kemp St. PE6 20 B4
Kennulphs Clo. PE6 20 C6
Leofric Clo. PE6 20 D5
Low Rd. PE6 20 A6
Manor Gdns. PE6 20 C4
Middle Rd. PE6 20 A5
Millfield Gdns. PE6 20 C4
Monks Mdw. PE6 20 B6
Nelson Clo. PE6 20 C4
Normanton Rd. PE6 20 B4
North Bank. PE6 20 B4
North St. PE6 20 B4
Pennald Clo. PE6 20 C6
Peterborough Rd. PE6 20 C6
Plank Drove. PE6 20 A6
Postland Rd. PE6 20 C6
Reform St. PE6 20 C5
St Benedict Clo. PE6 20 C5
St Guthlacs Clo. PE6 20 C5
St Marks Dri. PE6 20 B5
St Mary Clo. PE6 20 C5
St Pega Clo. PE6 20 C5
Second Drove. PE6 20 A4
Snowden Clo. PE6 20 C6
South St. PE6 20 C5
Stricklands Clo. PE6 20 C6
Tatwin Dri. PE6 20 C6
The Chase. PE6 20 C4
The Willows. PE6 20 B5
Thorney Rd. PE6 20 D6
Torfrida Clo. PE6 20 D4
Trinity Clo. PE6 20 B5

West Bank. PE6 20 B4
West St. PE6 20 B5
Wyche Av. PE6 20 C5

## DUNHOLME/ WELTON

Allwood Rd. LN2 25 D3
Anderson. LN2 25 D4
Ashing La. LN2 25 C2
Ayam Clo. LN2 25 C2
Barnes Wallis Ct. LN2 25 C2
Barrett Gro. LN2 25 D3
Beck La. LN2 25 F3
Beckhall. LN2 25 B3
Beech Clo. LN2 25 E4
Bishop Clo. LN2 25 E3
Bishops Pl. LN2 25 A2
Bramble Clo. LN2 25 C1
Brinkhall Way. LN2 25 C2
Chapel La. LN2 25 B2
Chapter Clo. LN2 25 A2
Church La. LN2 25 B2
Cliff Rd. LN2 25 B2
Cottingham Ct. LN2 25 D3
Deane Walk. LN2 25 D3
Dunholme Clo. LN2 25 D2
Dunholme Rd. LN2 25 D2
Eagle Dri. LN2 25 C1
Eastfield Clo. LN2 25 D2
Eastfield La. LN2 25 D2
Farm Vw. LN2 25 D1
Field Clo. LN2 25 B1
Furrow Clo. LN2 25 C3
Gorehall Dri. LN2 25 C1
Granthams. LN2 25 D4
Green La. LN2 25 B3
Greenway. LN2 25 B2
Hackthorn Rd. LN2 25 C1
Halfpenny Clo. LN2 25 D1
Hazel Gro. LN2 25 B2
Heath Clo. LN2 25 A2
Heath La. LN2 25 A2
Holmes La. LN2 25 E3
Honeyholes La. LN2 25 B4
Hughson Wk. LN2 25 D3
James Ct. LN2 25 B2
Keepers Clo. LN2 25 C1
Kennington Clo. LN2 25 D4
Kings Way. LN2 25 A2
Kneeland. LN2 25 D2
Lady Elizabeth Ct. LN2 25 E3
Lancaster Ct. LN2 25 B2
Lawson Ct. LN2 25 E3
Lincoln Rd,
 Dunholme. LN2 25 C4
Lincoln Rd,
 Welton. LN2 25 B2
Lodge Clo. LN2 25 C1
Mainwaring Clo. LN2 25 E3
*Manor Ct,
 Lincoln Rd. LN2 25 B2
Manor La. LN2 25 B2
Manor Way. LN2 25 E3
Market Rasen Rd. LN2 25 E3
Meadow Way. LN2 25 C2
Merleswen. LN2 25 D3
Monce Clo. LN2 25 D4
Monckton Way. LN2 25 D4
Morris Clo. LN2 25 D3
Musgraves Orch. LN2 25 D2
Norbeck La. LN2 25 B2
Northfield Rd. LN2 25 D2
Nursery Clo. LN2 25 E3
Oak Av. LN2 25 E3
Oak Vw. LN2 25 E4
Painshall Clo. LN2 25 C2
*Park House,
 Lincoln Rd. LN2 25 B2
Paynell. LN2 25 D3
Poachers Rest. LN2 25 B1
Pond Clo. LN2 25 C3
Prebend La. LN2 25 A1
Ridge Clo. LN2 25 C3
Rivehall Av. LN2 25 B2
Roselea Av. LN2 25 C2
Ryland Bri. LN2 25 D2
Ryland Gdns. LN2 25 D2
Ryland Rd,
 Dunholme. LN2 25 D2
Ryland Rd,
 Welton. LN2 25 B2
St Chads Ct. LN2 25 E3
St Marys Ct. LN2 25 B2

School Dri. LN2 25 B2
Scothern La. LN2 25 E3
Spring Clo. LN2 25 E3
Spring Ct. LN2 25 C2
Stonecliff Pk. LN2 25 A1
Sudbeck La. LN2 25 B3
Swan Clo. LN2 25 D3
Swen Clo. LN2 25 D1
Tennyson Dri. LN2 25 D3
The Carrs. LN2 25 C2
The Grove. LN2 25 C2
The Hardings. LN2 25 D2
The Harrows. LN2 25 C3
The Pastures. LN2 25 C2
The Spinneys. LN2 25 C1
The Wells. LN2 25 C2
Tinkermere Clo. LN2 25 C2
Vicarage La. LN2 25 B2
Watery La. LN2 25 E3
Wentworth Dri. LN2 25 D4
Westhall Rd. LN2 25 C2
Willow Way. LN2 25 C2
Woods End, LN2 25 D3

## GAINSBOROUGH

Acacia Av. DN21 26 C4
Acland St. DN21 27 B5
Adelaide Clo. DN21 27 E7
Aegir Clo. DN21 27 E7
Aisby Wk. DN21 27 E6
Albany St. DN21 26 B4
*Alec Rose Gro,
 Riseholme Rd. DN21 27 E7
Alfred St. DN21 26 B4
Anastasia Clo. DN21 26 B3
Apley Clo. DN21 27 E6
Arkwright St. DN21 26 C4
Arthur Rd. DN21 26 C4
Arundel Clo. DN21 26 D3
Ash Gro. DN21 26 D4
Ashcroft St. DN21 27 C7
Aspen Clo. DN21 26 E4
Asquith St. DN21 26 B4
Bacon St. DN21 27 C7
Baines Rd. DN21 27 E6
Balfour St. DN21 27 B5
Bayard St. DN21 27 B5
Beaufort St. DN21 26 B3
Beaumont St. DN21 27 C5
Beckett Av. DN21 26 D4
Beech Av. DN21 26 C4
Belvoir Clo. DN21 26 B2
Birch Gro. DN21 26 D4
Birrell St. DN21 26 B2
Blyton Rd. DN21 26 B2
Bowling Green Rd.
 DN21 27 B5
Bracken Clo. DN21 26 A3
Bramley Ct. DN21 26 E4
Bridge Rd. DN21 27 C7
Bridge St. DN21 27 C5
Bright St. DN21 27 C5
*Britannia Ter,
 Queen St. DN21 27 C6
Brocklesby Clo. DN21 27 E6
Burns St. DN21 26 A3
Burton St. DN21 27 C7
Bycroft St. DN21 26 B1
Cadman Way. DN21 27 F5
Caenby Clo. DN21 27 F6
Caldicott Dri. DN21 27 F6
Campbell St. DN21 26 B4
Carlisle St. DN21 26 C4
Carr La. DN21 27 B8
Carson Rd. DN21 26 C4
Caskgate St. DN21 27 B5
Cecil St. DN21 27 B5
Cedar Clo. DN21 26 A3
Chapel La. DN21 26 B2
Chapel Staith. DN21 27 B5
Charles St. DN21 26 C4
Cherry Tree Rd. DN21 27 E5
Chestnut Av. DN21 26 D4
*Church La,
 Parnell St. DN21 27 B5
Church St. DN21 26 C4
Claremont Rd. DN21 27 E7
Claythorne Dri. DN21 27 D6
Cleveland St. DN21 27 C6
Clinton Ter. DN21 27 C6
Cobden St. DN21 27 B5
Colville Ter. DN21 27 C6
Coningsby Clo. DN21 27 E6

Connaught Rd. DN21 26 C4
Corringham Rd. DN21 26 D4
Coxs Hill. DN21 27 C5
Cromwell St. DN21 27 C7
Crooked Billet St. DN21 26 A2
Cross St,
 Gainsborough. DN21 27 C5
Cross St, Morton. DN21 26 B2
Curzon St. DN21 26 B4
Danes Rd. DN21 27 E5
Darwin St. DN21 27 C7
*Dickenson Ter,
 Queen St. DN21 27 C6
Dog and Duck La.
 DN21 26 A2
Dorton Av. DN21 27 E6
Drake St. DN21 27 C7
Dunbar Clo. DN21 26 D4
Dunholme Clo. DN21 27 D6
Dunholme Rd. DN21 27 D6
Dunstall St. DN21 27 E6
Dunster Rd. DN21 26 D3
Eastern Av. DN21 27 E5
Edward Rd. DN21 26 C4
Elizabeth Clo. DN21 26 B3
Elsham Wk. DN21 27 F5
Enderby Cres. DN21 27 D6
Etherington St. DN21 27 C5
Fairfax Clo. DN21 27 E7
Fairway Av. DN21 26 B2
Fawcett St. DN21 27 B5
Field La. DN21 26 A1
Fillingham Clo. DN21 27 F7
*Flag Alley,
 Market Pl. DN21 27 C5
*Florence Ter,
 Sandsfield La. DN21 27 C6
Forster St. DN21 26 B4
Foxby Ct. DN21 27 E7
Foxby Hill. DN21 27 D8
*Frampton Ter,
 Queen St. DN21 27 C6
Francis Chichester Wk.
 DN21 27 E6
Front St. DN21 26 A2
Gainas Av. DN21 26 C4
Garfield St. DN21 26 B4
George St. DN21 26 A4
Gladstone St. DN21 27 B5
Glentham Rd. DN21 27 F7
Gordon St. DN21 27 C7
Granary Clo. DN21 26 B1
Grange Pk. DN21 26 A1
Grange Rd. DN21 27 F4
Grasby Clo. DN21 27 F7
Grasmere Clo. DN21 27 E4
Grey St. DN21 26 B4
Greystones Rd. DN21 26 A3
Hainton Clo. DN21 27 D6
Haldane St. DN21 26 B4
Haltham Grn. DN21 27 F5
Harpswell Clo. DN21 27 F7
Harrow Clo. DN21 26 E4
Hawthorn Av. DN21 26 C4
Hawthorn Gro. DN21 26 C4
Hawton Clo. DN21 26 D3
Heapham Cres. DN21 27 E5
Heapham Rd. DN21 27 D5
Heapham Rd Sth. DN21 27 F6
Heaton St. DN21 27 C5
Henley Ct. DN21 26 B4
Hickman Ct. DN21 27 D5
Hickman Cres. DN21 26 B1
Hickman St. DN21 27 C6
High St. DN21 27 C6
Highfield Clo. DN21 27 D5
Hill Cres. DN21 27 E5
Holme Walk. DN21 27 F5
Holme Wk. DN21 27 F5
Hotspur Rd. DN21 26 B3
Humble Carr La. DN21 27 C8
INDUSTRIAL & RETAIL:
Corringham Rd Ind Est.
 DN21 26 F4
Iona Clo. DN21 26 D4
Japan Rd. DN21 26 A4
Jubilee Cres. DN21 27 C5
Keelby Rd. DN21 27 F7
Kenmare Cres. DN21 27 E7
*Kexby Wk,
 Riseholme Rd. DN21 27 E7
King St. DN21 27 C6
Kingerby Clo. DN21 27 D6
Laburnum Av. DN21 26 D4
Larch Clo. DN21 26 E4
Laurel Clo. DN21 26 E4

Lea Rd. DN21 27 C7
Lewis St. DN21 27 C6
Limber Clo. DN21 27 F7
Lime Tree Av. DN21 26 C4
Lincoln St. DN21 26 B4
Linden Ter. DN21 27 C7
Linwood Clo. DN21 27 F7
Lissington Rd. DN21 27 D6
Long Wood. DN21 27 F5
Lord St. DN21 27 B5
Love La. DN21 26 B4
Ludford Cres. DN21 27 D6
Lusher Way. DN21 27 F5
Malpas Av. DN21 27 C5
Manor Rd. DN21 26 A2
Maple Clo. DN21 26 B3
Market Pl. DN21 27 C5
Market St. DN21 27 C5
Marlborough St. DN21 26 B4
Marlow Rd. DN21 26 D3
Marshall Way. DN21 27 F6
Mayfield Av. DN21 26 B3
Melrose Rd. DN21 26 B4
Melville St. DN21 27 C5
Mercer Rd. DN21 26 B4
Middlefield La. DN21 27 D5
Mill La. DN21 26 A1
Miller Rd. DN21 26 F4
Milton Rd. DN21 26 D3
Morley St. DN21 27 B5
Morton Clo. DN21 26 A2
Morton Rd. DN21 26 B2
Morton Ter. DN21 26 B3
Mowbray St. DN21 26 B4
Nelson St. DN21 27 C5
Newlands. DN21 27 D5
Newton Clo. DN21 27 F5
Noel St. DN21 26 B3
North Marsh Rd. DN21 26 B3
North Par. DN21 27 B5
North St,
 Gainsborough. DN21 26 C4
North St,
 Morton. DN21 26 B2
North Warren Rd.
 DN21 26 A3
Northolme. DN21 26 C4
Oak Tree Av. DN21 26 E4
Old Trent Rd. DN21 27 A5
Orchard Clo. DN21 26 B3
Park Springs Rd. DN21 27 E7
Parnell St. DN21 27 B5
Pasture Rd. DN21 27 E6
Pendeen Clo. DN21 26 D4
Pilham Ct. DN21 27 E7
Pillard Ho La. DN21 27 C6
Pingle Clo. DN21 27 D5
Pingle Hill. DN21 26 B4
Portland Ter. DN21 27 C6
Primrose St. DN21 27 C6
Princess Wk. DN21 27 E5
Priory Clo. DN21 27 E6
*Prospect Ter,
 Queen St. DN21 27 C6
Queen St. DN21 27 C6
Queensway. DN21 27 E5
Rachel Clo. DN21 26 B3
Ravendale Rd. DN21 27 D6
Rectory Av. DN21 27 C5
Redman Clo. DN21 26 E4
Riby Clo. DN21 27 F7
Richmond Rd. DN21 27 E5
Riseholme Rd. DN21 27 E7
Ropery Rd. DN21 26 A2
Rosefields. DN21 26 D4
Roseway. DN21 27 C5
Rothwell Clo. DN21 27 D6
Rowen Rd. DN21 26 E4
Rowston Clo. DN21 26 B4
Ruskin St. DN21 27 C7
St Johns Ter. DN21 27 C7
St Pauls Rd. DN21 26 A2
Salisbury Rd. DN21 26 B3
Sanders Rd. DN21 27 F6
Sandsfield La. DN21 27 C6
Saracen Clo. DN21 27 E7
Scampton Way. DN21 27 E7
Scott St. DN21 27 C5
Shakespeare St. DN21 27 D7
Silver St. DN21 27 C5
Somerby Rd. DN21 27 E5
South Par. DN21 27 E6
South St. DN21 26 B2
Southlands Av. DN21 26 B4
Southlands Dri. DN21 26 A1
Southlands Gdns.
 DN21 26 A1

Spital Hill. DN21 26 C4
Spital Ter. DN21 27 C5
Spring Gdns. DN21 27 C5
Springfield Clo. DN21 27 E5
Springthorpe Rd. DN21 27 E5
Stanley St. DN21 27 C7
Station Hill. DN21 27 C5
Stirling Clo. DN21 26 D4
Strafford St. DN21 27 C7
Sturgate Wk. DN21 27 E6
Summer Hill. DN21 26 D4
Summergangs La.
 DN21 27 B8
Swallow Clo. DN21 27 F7
Sycamore Dri. DN21 26 D4
Tealby Clo. DN21 27 F7
Tennyson St. DN21 27 C5
The Avenue. DN21 26 D3
The Belt. DN21 26 D3
The Drive. DN21 27 E6
The Flood Rd. DN21 27 A6
The Green. DN21 27 E6
The Little Belt. DN21 26 B2
The Pines. DN21 27 E7
The Precinct. DN21 27 E6
The Walk. DN21 27 E6
Theaker Av. DN21 27 C7
Thorndike Way. DN21 27 C7
Thorndyke Mws. DN21 27 C6
Thornton St. DN21 27 C6
Thurlby Rd. DN21 27 C6
Tooley St. DN21 27 C6
Torr St. DN21 27 C6
Tower St. DN21 27 C5
Trent St. DN21 27 C7
Trentside. DN21 26 A2
Trinity Clo. DN21 27 C6
Trinity St. DN21 27 C6
Tudor Dri. DN21 26 A2
Turpin Clo. DN21 26 E4
Ulster Rd. DN21 26 C4
Upton Wk. DN21 27 E6
Vanessa Dri. DN21 26 B2
Victoria Clo. DN21 27 E7
Walkerith Rd. DN21 26 A1
Wall St. DN21 27 C6
Warren Clo. DN21 26 A3
Washington St. DN21 27 C7
Waterworks St. DN21 27 C7
Wellington St. DN21 27 C7
Wembley St. DN21 27 C6
West St. DN21 26 B2
*Wheeldon St,
 Queen St. DN21 27 C6
Whites Wood La. DN21 27 D5
Willoughby St. DN21 27 C6
Willow Clo. DN21 26 A3
Wilson St. DN21 26 A4
Wintern Ct. DN21 27 C7
Woodfield Rd. DN21 27 D5
Woodhill Av. DN21 26 D4
Woodland Av. DN21 26 B2
Woods Ter. DN21 26 B3

## GRANTHAM

Abbeydale Cres. NG31 28 C4
Abraham Clo. NG31 29 H1
Acorn Clo. NG31 29 E4
Adamstyles. NG32 30 A2
Agnes St. NG31 31 F2
Aire Rd. NG31 30 D4
Albert St. NG31 31 G4
Albion Pl. NG31 31 F1
Albion Rd. NG31 31 F1
Albion St. NG31 28 C6
Alexandra Rd. NG31 31 F1
Alford St. NG31 31 F1
Alma Park Clo. NG31 29 H5
Alma Park Rd. NG31 31 H4
Almond Gro. NG31 29 E5
Ambergate Wk. NG31 30 D3
Anson St. NG31 31 H4
Applewood Clo. NG31 28 B3
Arnold Av. NG31 28 B3
Arnold Field Ct. NG31 28 B3
Ascot Dri. NG31 29 F4
Ash Gro. NG31 29 F5
Ashley Dri. NG31 28 B3
Avenue Rd. NG31 31 F2
Aviary Clo. NG31 29 E6
Avon Clo. NG31 30 D3
Balmoral Dri. NG31 30 C1
Barnwell Ter. NG31 31 E3

**68**

Turnpike Clo. NG31 30 C5
Tyndal Rd. NG31 31 E1
Tyson Clo. NG31 29 E5
Union St. NG31 31 E2
Uplands Dri. NG31 29 F6
Vale Rd. NG31 28 B4
Valley Rd. NG31 30 B2
Ventnor Av. NG31 30 C2
Venture Way. NG31 30 C4
Vernon Av. NG31 28 B3
Victoria St. NG31 31 F4
Vine St. NG31 31 F2
Vivian Clo. NG31 28 B3
Wakefield Clo. NG31 30 B2
Walton Gdns. NG31 31 F4
Walton Heath Clo. NG31 29 F4
Wardour Dri. NG31 29 H6
Warren Way. NG31 29 H4
Warwick Clo. NG31 30 C2
Watergate. NG31 31 F2
Webster Way. NG31 28 B4
Welby Gdns. NG31 31 F1
Welby St. NG31 31 F2
Welham St. NG31 31 F2
Welland Ct. NG31 30 D4
Wellington Dri. NG31 31 H4
Wells Clo. NG31 30 B1
Welwyn Clo. NG31 30 C5
Wensleydale Clo. NG31 28 C3
Wentworth Dri. NG31 29 F4
West Av. NG31 30 C3
Westbourne Pl. NG31 30 D2
Westerdale Rd. NG31 28 C4
Westgate. NG31 31 E3
Westminster Way. NG31 30 D1
Westside Av. NG31 30 C6
Wharf Rd. NG31 31 F3
*William St, Commercial Rd. NG31 31 F3
Willow La. NG31 30 D5
Winchester Rd. NG31 30 C2
Windsor Dri. NG31 29 G6
Witham Rd. NG31 31 F2
Withambrook Pk. NG31 29 H4
Woburn Dri. NG31 29 H6
Woffindin Clo. NG31 28 A3
Wong Gdns. NG32 30 B6
Woodlands Dri. NG31 31 G2
Worcester Rd. NG31 30 C1
Wordsworth Clo. NG31 29 G6
Wroxall Dri. NG31 30 C2
Wyndham Clo. NG31 31 G1
Wyville Rd. NG31 30 C6
Yarmouth Av. NG31 30 C3
York Way. NG31 30 B2

## GRIMSBY

Abbey Dri East. DN32 32 D6
Abbey Dri West. DN32 32 D6
Abbey Park Mews. DN32 32 D6
Abbey Park Rd. DN32 32 D6
Abbey Rd. DN32 32 D6
Abbey Walk. DN31 33 E5
Abbotsway. DN32 32 D6
Acklam Gro. DN32 33 G6
Adam Smith St. DN31 32 C3
Ainslie St. DN32 33 E6
Albert St East. DN32 33 F3
Albert St West. DN32 33 F3
Albion St. DN32 33 F4
Alexandra Rd. DN31 32 D5
Alfred St. DN31 32 D4
Alfred Ter. DN32 32 D6
Allenby Av. DN34 32 B6
Anderson St. DN31 32 D5
Annesly St. DN31 32 D3
Ariston St. DN32 33 H5
Armstrong Pl East. DN31 32 C3
Armstrong Pl West. DN31 32 C3
Armstrong St. DN31 32 C3
Arthur St. DN31 32 C5
Arundel Wk. DN34 32 A5
Ashtree Av. DN34 32 A6
Auckland Rd. DN31 33 F2
Augusta St. DN34 32 C6
Ayscough St. DN31 32 D4
Balmoral Av. DN34 32 B5
Barcroft St. DN35 33 H5
Bargate. DN34 32 D6
Barnett Pl. DN35 33 H5
Baroness Ct. DN34 32 A6
Baroness Rd. DN34 32 A6
Bath St. DN32 33 G3
Baytree Av. DN34 32 A6
Bedford St. DN32 33 G4
Beechfield Ct. DN34 32 C6
Beeson Gro. DN31 32 C4
Beeson St. DN31 32 C4
Bemrose Way. DN31 32 C5
Bethlehem St. DN31 32 D5
Birch Av. DN34 32 A6
Birchin Way. DN31 32 B3
Bishops Wk. DN34 32 C6
Bodiam Way. DN32 33 F4
Boulevard Av. DN31 32 B5
Bowers Av. DN31 32 B5
Bradley St. DN32 33 E5
Bradman Ct. DN32 33 G3
Brereton Av. DN35 33 H4
Bridge Gdns. DN31 32 B3
Bridge St Nth. DN32 33 F3
Brighowgate. DN32 32 D6
Browns Orch. DN32 32 D6
Bull Ring La. DN31 32 D5
Buller St. DN32 33 F5
Butler Pl. DN35 33 H5
Buttermere Way. DN32 33 F4
Canterbury Dri. DN34 32 C6
Carlton Rd. DN34 32 C6
Carr La. DN35 33 H5
Carson Av. DN34 32 B6
Cartergate. DN31 32 D6
Cartledge Av. DN32 33 G6
Cartmel Gro. DN32 33 H6
Casswell Clo. DN32 33 G4
Castle St. DN32 33 G4
Catherine St. DN32 33 E6
Cavendish Way. DN32 33 F5
Central Par. DN34 32 A6
Chantry La. DN31 32 C5
Chapman Ct. DN31 32 D4
Charles Hume Ct. DN32 33 H4
Charlton St. DN31 32 C4
Chelmsford Av. DN34 32 B6
Chelmsford Pl. DN34 32 B6
Chestnut Av. DN31 32 C5
Church La. DN31 32 D5
Church St. DN32 33 F3
Churchill Way. DN32 33 F5
Clark Av. DN31 32 B5
Clavering St. DN31 32 B3
Cleethorpe Rd. DN31 33 E3
Clerke St. DN35 33 H4
Cleveland Gdns. DN31 32 B3
Cleveland St. DN31 32 B3
Clifton Rd. DN34 32 B6
Colin Av. DN32 33 H6
College St. DN34 32 C6
Colson Pl. DN35 33 H5
Columbia Rd. DN32 33 G6
Comber Pl. DN32 33 F4
Compton Dri. DN34 32 C6
Convamore Rd. DN32 33 F5
Conway Av. DN34 32 A5
Cooper Rd. DN32 33 G6
Corinthian Av. DN34 32 B6
Corporation Rd. DN31 32 C4
Craven Rd. DN35 33 H5
Crescent St. DN31 32 C5
Cressy St. DN31 33 E3
Cromwell Rd. DN31 32 A4
Cross Coates Rd. DN34 32 A6
Cross St. DN31 33 F2
*Cyril Cooper Ct, Abbey Dri East. DN32 32 D6
Daubney St. DN35 33 H5
Davie Pl. DN35 33 H5
Deansgate. DN31 32 D6
Derby Clo. DN32 33 G4
Dial Sq. DN31 33 E5
Donnington St. DN32 33 F5
Doughty Rd. DN32 33 E5
Douglas Av. DN31 32 B5
Dover St. DN31 32 D5
Duchess St. DN32 32 D6
Dudley St. DN31 32 C5
Dugard Rd. DN35 33 H5
Duke St. DN32 33 G4
Duncombe Gdns. DN32 33 F4
Duncombe St. DN32 33 F4
Dunmow St. DN31 32 C5
Durban Rd. DN32 33 G6
Durham Av. DN34 32 A5
Earl St. DN31 32 C5
East Gate. DN32 33 E5
East Marsh St. DN32 33 E4
East St Marys Gate. DN31 32 D5
East St. DN31 33 E5
Eastside Rd. DN31 33 F3
Edmonds Way. DN31 32 D4
Edward St. DN32 33 F5
Eleanor St. DN32 33 F5
Ellis Way. DN31 33 E5
Elm Av. DN34 32 A6
Elsenham Rd. DN31 32 B3
Enterprise Way. DN32 33 G6
Escart Rd. DN32 33 H6
Estate Rd No. 1. DN31 32 A2
Estate Rd No. 2. DN31 32 A3
Estate Rd No. 3. DN31 32 A2
Estate Rd No. 5. DN31 32 A2
Estuary Way. DN31 32 B2
Evelyn Gro Nth. DN32 33 H6
Evelyn Gro Sth. DN32 33 H6
Fairfax Rd. DN34 32 B5
Fairmont Rd. DN32 33 G6
Farebrother St. DN32 33 E6
Faringdon Rd. DN31 33 G2
Felstead Rd. DN34 32 A6
Fildes St. DN31 32 D5
Fircroft Way. DN34 32 B5
Fish Dock Rd. DN31 33 F3
Fishermans Wharf. DN31 32 D4
Flour Sq. DN31 33 E3
Fotheaby St. DN31 33 E4
Fraser St. DN32 33 F5
Frederick St. DN31 32 D4
Frederick Ward Way. DN31 32 D5
Freeman St. DN32 33 F5
Freeston St. DN35 33 H5
Freshney Dri. DN31 32 D4
Freshney Pl. DN31 32 D5
Garden St. DN31 32 D5
Garibaldi St. DN32 33 F4
Garth La. DN31 32 D5
Gate Way. DN31 32 C2
George Janney Ct. DN32 33 F4
Georges St. DN31 33 E5
Gilbey Rd. DN31 32 B2
Gorton St. DN31 33 F3
Gosport Rd. DN34 32 A6
Grafton St. DN32 33 G4
Grange Wk. DN34 32 A6
Grant St. DN35 33 H3
Granville St. DN32 33 F6
Grime St. DN31 33 E4
Grimsby Rd. DN35 33 H4
Grosvenor Cres. DN32 32 D6
Grosvenor St. DN32 32 D6
Grove Cres. DN32 33 H6
Guildford St. DN32 33 G4
Hainton Av. DN32 33 E6
Hamilton St. DN32 33 G3
Hamont Rd. DN32 33 H6
Hare St. DN32 33 F6
Hargrave St. DN31 32 C5
Harlech Way. DN32 33 F4
Harlow St. DN31 32 B3
Harold St. DN32 33 G4
Harrington St. DN35 33 H3
Harrison St. DN31 32 C5
Haven Av. DN31 32 C4
Haven Gdns. DN31 32 B3
Hawkins Gro. DN32 33 H6
Haycroft Av. DN31 32 C5
Haycroft St. DN31 32 C5
Helene Gro. DN32 33 H6
Heneage Rd. DN32 33 F6
Henry St. DN31 32 C4
Hilda St. DN32 33 G3
Hildyard St. DN32 33 G4
Holme St. DN32 33 E5
Holyoake Rd. DN32 33 H6
Hope St. DN32 33 F4
Huddleston Rd. DN32 33 G6
Humber Bank Sth. DN31 33 G2
Humber Bridge. DN31 33 G3
Humber Bridge Rd. DN31 33 G3
Humber St. DN31 33 G3
Humberstone Rd. DN32 33 G5
Hume St. DN31 32 C5
Hutton Rd. DN31 33 F2

**INDUSTRIAL & RETAIL:**
Abbeygate Shopping Centre. DN31 32 D5
Acorn Business Centre. DN31 33 E6
Alexandra Retail Pk. DN31 32 D4
Birchin Way Ind Est. DN31 32 B3
Europa Business Pk. DN31 32 B2
High Point Retail Pk. DN31 33 E3
South Humberside Ind Est. DN31 32 A3
Venture Business Pk. DN31 32 B2
West Marsh Ind Est. DN31 32 D4

Intax Farm Mews. DN32 33 F6
Jackson St. DN31 32 C4
James St. DN31 32 C4
Jenner Pl. DN35 33 H5
Johnson St. DN35 33 H4
Joseph St. DN31 32 C4
Julian St. DN32 33 F5
Kathleen Gro. DN32 33 H6
Kemp Rd. DN31 33 G1
Kent St. DN32 33 F3
King Edward St. DN31 33 E4
Kingston Av. DN34 32 B6
Kirmington Gdns. DN34 32 A6
Knight St. DN32 33 H6
Ladysmith Rd. DN32 33 F5
Lambert Rd. DN32 32 D6
Lampton Gro. DN32 33 E6
Lampton Rd. DN32 33 E6
Lancaster Av. DN31 32 C5
Landeck Av. DN34 32 B6
Lawrence St. DN31 32 C4
Lawson Av. DN31 32 C5
Legsby Av. DN32 33 E6
Lichfield Rd. DN32 33 H6
Limber Ct. DN34 32 A6
Limber Vale. DN34 32 A6
Lime St. DN31 32 C5
Lincoln Av. DN31 32 C5
Lister St. DN31 32 C4
Little Michael St. DN34 32 C5
Littlefield La. DN34 32 B6
Lockhill. DN31 33 E3
Lombard St. DN34 32 B5
Lord St. DN31 32 C4
Lovett St. DN35 33 H5
Lower Burgess St. DN31 33 E4
Lower Spring St. DN31 33 E3
Ludford St. DN32 33 E6
Ludlow Av. DN34 32 A5
Macaulay St. DN31 32 B4
Maclure St. DN31 33 F2
Mallard Mews. DN32 33 E6
Malmesbury Dri. DN34 32 C6
Maltings Way. DN31 33 E4
Mandela Link. DN31 32 C5
Manningtree Clo. DN32 33 E6
Manor Av. DN32 32 D6
Manor Ct. DN32 32 D6
Mansel St. DN32 33 H4
Marcus St. DN34 32 A6
Market St. DN31 33 E4
Marklew Av. DN34 32 B5
Marsden Rd. DN31 33 G3
Marshall Av. DN34 32 B6
*Middle Ct, Upper Burgess St. DN31 33 E4
Mill Av. DN31 32 C4
Miller Av. DN35 33 H6
Millom Way. DN32 33 F4
Montague St. DN35 33 H4
Moody La. DN31 32 A1
Morpeth Wk. DN34 32 A6
Morton Rd. DN34 32 B5
Moss Rd. DN32 33 E6
Murray St. DN31 33 F3
Nacton St. DN31 33 F3
Naseby Dri. DN31 32 B5
Naseby Gro. DN31 32 B5
Nelson St. DN32 33 F4
New Cartergate. DN31 32 D5
New Haven Ter. DN31 32 B3
New St. DN31 33 E5
Newby Rd. DN31 32 C5
Newmarket St. DN32 33 F4
Newsham Dri. DN34 32 A6
Norman Rd. DN34 32 B5
North Quay. DN31 33 G1
Old Market Pl. DN31 32 D5
Oliver Ct. DN31 32 D4
Orwell St. DN31 33 F3
Osborne St. DN31 32 D5
Oxford St. DN32 33 F4
Park St. DN35 33 H4
Park View. DN35 33 H5
Pasture St. DN31 33 E5
Peaks Parkway. DN32 33 E5
Pelham Rd. DN34 32 C6
Pembroke Av. DN34 32 A5
Peppercorn Wk. DN32 33 E6
Petchell Way. DN32 33 F4
Phelps St. DN35 33 H4
Phyllis Av. DN34 32 C6
Prince Albert Gdns. DN31 33 E3
Princess Av. DN31 32 C5
Pyewipe Rd. DN31 32 C2
Queen Mary Av. DN35 33 H5
Queen St. DN31 33 E5
Queens Par. DN31 32 C5
Railway Pl. DN31 33 F3
Railway St. DN32 33 E4
Rendell St. DN31 32 D4
Riby Sq. DN31 33 F3
Riby St. DN31 33 F3
Richard St. DN31 32 C4
Richmond Rd. DN34 32 B6
Ripon St. DN31 32 C5
Roberts St. DN32 33 F5
Robinson La. DN31 33 G3
Robinson St East. DN32 33 E5
Ropery St. DN32 33 F6
Rosalind Av. DN34 32 C5
Roseveare Av. DN31 32 B5
Rosina Gro Nth. DN32 33 H6
Rosina Gro Sth. DN32 33 H6
Ross Rd. DN31 33 G3
Royal St. DN31 33 E3
Runswick Rd. DN32 33 G6
Rutland Ct. DN32 33 G5
Rutland St. DN32 33 G5
Sackville St. DN34 32 C6
St Albans Av. DN31 32 B5
St Anns Av. DN34 32 C6
St Francis Av. DN31 32 B5
St Hildas Av. DN34 32 C6
St James Av. DN34 32 A6
St James Ct. DN34 32 C6
St Leonards Av. DN31 32 B4
St Lukes Ct. DN32 33 F5
St Mawes Cres. DN34 32 A5
St Olafs Gro. DN32 33 E6
Salamander Clo. DN31 32 C4
Salisbury Av. DN34 32 B6
Salmeston Ct. DN34 32 C6
Salvesen Rd. DN31 33 H3
Samuel Av. DN32 33 H6
Sanders St. DN31 32 C5
Sandford St. DN31 32 C5
Saxon Ct. DN31 32 B2
Sheepfold St. DN32 33 E5
Sidney Pl. DN35 33 H4
Sidney Rd. DN34 32 B5
Sidney St. DN35 33 H4
Sidney Way. DN35 33 H4
Sixhills St. DN32 33 E5
Somersby St. DN31 32 D5
South Par. DN31 32 D4
South View. DN34 32 A6
Spark St. DN34 32 B5
Spencer St. DN31 33 H3
Spring Bank. DN34 32 A5
Springway Cres. DN34 32 A5
Stanley St. DN32 33 G5
Stirling St. DN31 33 G3
Stortford St. DN31 32 B3
Strand St. DN32 33 F3
Stuart Wortley St. DN31 33 F2
Surtees St. DN31 33 F2
Sussex St. DN35 33 H4
Tasburgh St. DN32 33 F6
Taylor St. DN35 33 H3
Telford Pl. DN34 32 A5
Tenby Wk. DN34 32 B5
Tennyson St. DN31 32 D4
Tewkesbury Ct. DN34 32 C6
The Close. DN34 32 C6
The Drawing Ct. DN31 32 B2
The Lanes. DN34 32 C6

The Spinney. DN34    32 C6
The Square. DN32    33 G4
Thesiger St. DN32    33 F4
Thornhill Gdns. DN34    32 A5
Thorold St. DN31    33 G3
Tom Hammond Way.
   DN32    33 F4
Tomline St. DN31    33 F3
Toothill Gdns. DN34    32 A6
Toothill Rd. DN34    32 A6
Town Hall Sq. DN31    33 E5
Town Hall St. DN31    33 E5
Trinity St. DN31    33 G3
Tunnard St. DN32    33 G4
Tyler Av. DN31    32 B5
Upper Burgess St.
   DN31    33 E4
Upper Burgess St.
   DN31    33 E5
Upper Spring St. DN31    33 E5
Veal St. DN31    32 C5
Vicarage Gdns. DN34    32 C6
Vicarage Lawn. DN34    32 C6
Victor St. DN32    33 F4
Victoria Ct. DN31    33 E4
Victoria St Nth. DN31    33 E4
Victoria St Sth. DN31    33 E4
Victoria St West. DN31    33 E4
Wall St. DN34    32 B5
Waterside Dri. DN31    32 D4
Watkin St Nth. DN31    32 D3
Watkin St Sth. DN31    32 D4
Weelsby St. DN32    33 G5
Weelsby St Sth. DN32    33 G5
Welholme Av. DN32    32 D6
Welholme Rd. DN32    33 F6
Wellington St. DN32    33 F4
Wellowgate. DN32    32 D6
Wellowgate Mews.
   DN32    32 D6
Wells St. DN31    32 D5
Wentworth Rd. DN34    32 B5
Werneth Rd. DN32    32 C3
West Coates Rd. DN31    32 C3
West St Marys Gate.
   DN31    32 D5
Westgate. DN31    32 D3
Westminster Dri. DN34    32 C6
Westside Rd. DN31    32 C2
Wharncliffe Rd Nth.
   DN31    33 F1
Wharton St. DN31    32 C5
Wickham Rd. DN31    33 G3
Willing Way. DN32    33 F4
Willingham St. DN32    33 E6
Wimborn Av. DN34    32 B6
Winceby Av. DN31    32 B5
Winston Av. DN34    32 B5
Wintringham Rd. DN32    33 E6
Womersley Rd. DN31    33 G3
Wood St. DN32    33 F4
Wragby St. DN32    33 F5
Yarborough Dri. DN31    32 D4
Yarborough Rd. DN34    32 A6
Yarrow Rd. DN34    32 A5
York St. DN31    32 C4
Young Pl. DN35    33 H5

## HECKINGTON

Allison Rd. NG34    34 B2
Banks La. NG34    34 B2
Barley Clo. NG34    34 A2
Beckett Clo. NG34    34 A2
Beech Clo. NG34    34 A1
Boston Rd. NG34    34 C2
Bramley Clo. NG34    34 B2
Burton Rd. NG34    34 A2
Cameron St. NG34    34 B2
Christopher Clo. NG34    34 B1
Church St. NG34    34 B1
Churchill Way. NG34    34 B1
Churchview Clo. NG34    34 B1
Cobham Clo. NG34    34 C2
Colby Way. NG34    34 B1
Cowgate. NG34    34 B1
Eastgate. NG34    34 B1
Foster St. NG34    34 B1
Godson Av. NG34    34 A1
Hale Rd. NG34    34 A3
Hall Clo. NG34    34 A2
Handley St. NG34    34 B1
Hare Clo. NG34    34 A3
Heckington By-Pass.
   NG34    34 C1

High St. NG34    34 B2
Houlden Way. NG34    34 B1
Howell Rd. NG34    34 B1
Hubbard Clo. NG34    34 A1
Ingledew Clo. NG34    34 C3
Kyme Rd. NG34    34 C1
Lambourne Way. NG34    34 B2
Latimer Gdns. NG34    34 C2
Laxton Clo. NG34    34 B2
Limetree Wk. NG34    34 B2
Manor St. NG34    34 B1
Maple Gro. NG34    34 A1
Mayflower Dri. NG34    34 A2
Millers Way. NG34    34 C3
Millview Rd. NG34    34 C3
Nash Clo. NG34    34 C3
New St. NG34    34 C2
Norris Clo. NG34    34 B2
Oak Way. NG34    34 A2
Oatfield Way. NG34    34 A2
Orchard Dri. NG34    34 C2
Osborn Way. NG34    34 A2
Pocklington Way. NG34    34 C3
Potesgrave Way.
   NG34    34 A1
Richards Clo. NG34    34 B2
Royal Oak Ct. NG34    34 C2
St Andrews St. NG34    34 B2
Scoggins Way. NG34    34 A1
Shrubwood Clo. NG34    34 B2
Skelton Clo. NG34    34 B2
Sleaford Rd. NG34    34 A2
Station Rd. NG34    34 C2
Stirling Ct. NG34    34 A2
Vicarage Rd. NG34    34 C1
Wellington Way. NG34    34 C2
Willow Clo. NG34    34 A3
Windmill Dri. NG34    34 C3
Woodmans Clo. NG34    34 A1

## HOLBEACH

Albert St. PE12    35 B3
Albert Wk. PE12    35 D4
Albion St. PE12    35 F3
Alison Av. PE12    35 F3
All Saints Clo. PE12    35 E2
Angell La. PE12    35 D4
Armitage Clo. PE12    35 F3
Arthurs Av. PE12    35 C4
Ash Clo. PE12    35 C2
Back La. PE12    35 C3
Back St. PE12    35 C3
Balmoral Way. PE12    35 F2
Barretts Clo. PE12    35 D4
Barrington Clo. PE12    35 D4
Barrington Gate. PE12    35 D4
Battlefields La Nth.
   PE12    35 F2
Battlefields La Sth.
   PE12    35 D3
Boston Rd Nth. PE12    35 C2
Boston Rd Sth. PE12    35 C2
Branches La. PE12    35 F3
Broome Way. PE12    35 A4
Bush Meadow La. PE12    35 A2
Cackle Hill La. PE12    35 B1
Castle Dri. PE12    35 E4
Cecil Pywell Av. PE12    35 C2
Cedar Dri. PE12    35 B2
Chancery La. PE12    35 D4
Chapel St. PE12    35 D3
Cherry Tree La. PE12    35 C2
Chestnut Av. PE12    35 C2
Church St. PE12    35 D3
Church Wk. PE12    35 D4
Coles Clo. PE12    35 E2
College Clo. PE12    35 B3
Cornfields. PE12    35 B3
Cranmore La. PE12    35 B4
Creewood Clo. PE12    35 B4
Cross St, Fleet. PE12    35 F4
Cross St,
   Holbeach. PE12    35 D3
Dam Gate. PE12    35 E4
Drakes Clo. PE12    35 E4
East Elloe Av. PE12    35 C3
Edinburgh Wk. PE12    35 F2
Fairfields. PE12    35 B3
Fakenham Chase. PE12    35 D2
Farmers Gate. PE12    35 D2
Farrow Av. PE12    35 D4
Fen Rd. PE12    35 B4
Fenland Way. PE12    35 B3

Fishpond La. PE12    35 D4
Fleet Rd. PE12    35 E3
Fleet Rd Ind Est. PE12    35 F3
Fleet St. PE12    35 D3
Foxes Low Rd. PE12    35 E3
Greenfields. PE12    35 E3
Hall Gate. PE12    35 B4
Hall Hill Rd. PE12    35 C4
Harwood Av. PE12    35 B4
Heridian Walk. PE12    35 B4
High St. PE12    35 D3
Hix Clo. PE12    35 B3
Holland Way. PE12    35 B4
Hungerdike Gate. PE12    35 A3
Hunters Clo. PE12    35 D4
Huntingdon Clo. PE12    35 D2
**INDUSTRIAL & RETAIL:**
Fleet Rd Ind Est. PE12    35 F3
Isaac Newtons Clo.
   PE12    35 B4
Kennedy Rd. PE12    35 B1
Kensington Gdns. PE12    35 F2
King George V Av.
   PE12    35 E2
Kings Rd. PE12    35 F3
Kingston Gdns. PE12    35 F2
Langwith Dri. PE12    35 B4
Langwith Gdns. PE12    35 C4
Lawrence Clo. PE12    35 A4
Lime Gro. PE12    35 C2
Littlebury Gdns. PE12    35 C3
Low La. PE12    35 E2
Lyndis Wk. PE12    35 E4
Manor Dri. PE12    35 C2
Maple Gro. PE12    35 A4
Market Rasen. PE12    35 E3
Marshlands Dri. PE12    35 E3
Mattimore Dri. PE12    35 E3
Mill La. PE12    35 A1
Mondemont Clo. PE12    35 D3
Netherfield. PE12    35 B3
North Par. PE12    35 E3
Northons La. PE12    35 B2
Oakwood Glade. PE12    35 B2
Park Gdns. PE12    35 D2
Park La. PE12    35 D3
Park Rd. PE12    35 D3
Pearl Ct. PE12    35 C3
Penny Hill Rd. PE12    35 D1
Pine Clo. PE12    35 C2
Princes St. PE12    35 F3
Rathkenny Clo. PE12    35 E4
Reapers Clo. PE12    35 B3
Rowan Clo. PE12    35 C2
St Catherine Ct. PE12    35 D3
St John St. PE12    35 D3
St Matthew Clo. PE12    35 C4
St William Ct. PE12    35 D4
Sandringham Clo. PE12    35 F3
Spalding Rd. PE12    35 A3
Spencer Gdns. PE12    35 F2
Spruce Clo. PE12    35 B2
Station Rd. PE12    35 D4
Stockmans Av. PE12    35 E2
Stockwell Gate East.
   PE12    35 A1
Stukeley Dri. PE12    35 C3
Stukeley Gdns. PE12    35 C3
Stukeley Rd. PE12    35 C4
The Boundaries. PE12    35 C4
The Brambles. PE12    35 E3
The Close. PE12    35 D3
The Hollies. PE12    35 E3
The Laurels. PE12    35 A4
The Paddocks. PE12    35 D2
The Sidings. PE12    35 C4
The Tenters. PE12    35 C3
Tolls La. PE12    35 D1
Union St. PE12    35 F3
Victoria St. PE12    35 D3
Washway Rd. PE12    35 E1
Waterside Gdns. PE12    35 A3
Welbourne La. PE12    35 B1
Welbourne La East.
   PE12    35 C2
Welbourne La West.
   PE12    35 B2
Welby Gdns. PE12    35 A3
West End. PE12    35 D3
Western Av. PE12    35 B3
Wheatsheaf Clo. PE12    35 E3
Wignals Gate. PE12    35 A4
Wilders Garth. PE12    35 E3
Windmill Clo. PE12    35 B4
Windsor Av. PE12    35 E3

## HORNCASTLE

Accommodation Rd.
   LN9    36 C2
Albert St. LN9    36 E3
Ancaster Ct. LN9    36 D3
Ashwood Clo. LN9    36 C2
Baggaley Dri. LN9    36 B2
Banks Rd. LN9    36 E2
Banks St. LN9    36 D3
Banovallum Gdns. LN9    36 F3
Bargate La. LN9    36 E3
Barley Way. LN9    36 C3
Bonnetable Rd. LN9    36 E3
Boston Rd. LN9    36 D3
Bowl Alley La. LN9    36 E2
Bridge St. LN9    36 E4
Brook Rd. LN9    36 E4
Bryant Clo. LN9    36 D3
Burton Way. LN9    36 F4
Cagthorpe. LN9    36 D3
Carlisle Gdns. LN9    36 E1
Chestnut Clo. LN9    36 C1
Church La. LN9    36 D3
Churchill Av. LN9    36 D4
College Clo. LN9    36 E4
College Pk. LN9    36 E4
Conging St. LN9    36 D2
Corn Clo. LN9    36 D2
Coronation Wk. LN9    36 C3
Croft St. LN9    36 D4
Cromwell Av. LN9    36 D4
Cross St. LN9    36 E3
Dovecote All. LN9    36 D2
Dymoke Clo. LN9    36 D4
East St. LN9    36 D3
Elmhirst Rd. LN9    36 C1
Elsom Way. LN9    36 C2
Fairfax Clo. LN9    36 F3
Fleece Ct. LN9    36 D2
Foundry St. LN9    36 E3
Gas St. LN9    36 E3
Granary Way. LN9    36 C3
Hammerton La. LN9    36 E1
Harrison Clo. LN9    36 E1
Hazel Clo. LN9    36 C1
Hemingby Rd. LN9    36 D1
Hemingby Way. LN9    36 D1
High St. LN9    36 D2
Holly Clo. LN9    36 F4
Holmes Way. LN9    36 F4
Holt La. LN9    36 D3
Hopton St. LN9    36 D3
Islip Ct. LN9    36 E3
Jessop Clo. LN9    36 E3
Jobson Rd. LN9    36 E4
John Brown Clo. LN9    36 C2
Jubilee Way. LN9    36 C3
Lancaster Av. LN9    36 E2
Langton Clo. LN9    36 B3
Langton Dri. LN9    36 B3
Langton Hill. LN9    36 B3
Langton La. LN9    36 A2
Lincoln Rd. LN9    36 B1
Linden Rd. LN9    36 D2
*Lindsey Ct,
   Wharf Rd. LN9    36 D3
Lodington Ct. LN9    36 F3
Lord Raglan Ter. LN9    36 E3
Louth Rd. LN9    36 E2
Low Toynton Clo. LN9    36 E2
Low Toynton Rd. LN9    36 E1
Madely Clo. LN9    36 D4
Manor Ho St. LN9    36 D3
Maple Clo. LN9    36 C1
Mareham Rd. LN9    36 D3
Mark Av. LN9    36 C1
Market Pl. LN9    36 D2
Mill La. LN9    36 D2
Millstone Clo. LN9    36 C3
Millview Clo. LN9    36 D2
Ndola Dri. LN9    36 D4
North St. LN9    36 D2
*Old Paddock Ct,
   Conging St. LN9    36 D2
Orchard Way. LN9    36 C2
Osborne Way. LN9    36 D4
*Paradise Pl,
   Foundry St. LN9    36 E3
*Paradise Row,
   Foundry St. LN9    36 E3
Park Rd. LN9    36 E2
Prospect St. LN9    36 D2

Queen St. LN9    36 D3
Reindeer Clo. LN9    36 C2
Roman Way. LN9    36 F3
*St Lawrence St,
   High St. LN9    36 D2
St Marys Sq. LN9    36 D3
Saxon Way. LN9    36 F3
Sellwood Gdns. LN9    36 D3
South St. LN9    36 D3
Southfield Pl. LN9    36 D4
Southwells La. LN9    36 D2
Spilsby Rd. LN9    36 E3
Spratt Clo. LN9    36 F4
Stanhope Rd. LN9    36 E2
Stanhope Ter. LN9    36 E2
Station La. LN9    36 C3
Stonewell Row. LN9    36 D2
Stourton St. LN9    36 C2
Tennyson Gdns. LN9    36 E4
The Becks. LN9    36 E2
The Crescent. LN9    36 E2
The Gardens. LN9    36 D3
The Sidings. LN9    36 D3
The Wong. LN9    36 D3
Thimbleby Hill. LN9    36 A2
Thomas Gibson Dri.
   LN9    36 E3
Thomas Scully Clo.
   LN9    36 C2
Thornton Cres. LN9    36 D4
Tudor Pk. LN9    36 E2
Tweed Clo. LN9    36 F4
Upland Clo. LN9    36 C2
Waring St. LN9    36 D3
Watermill Rd. LN9    36 E4
Wesley Way. LN9    36 E4
West St. LN9    36 C2
Wharf Rd. LN9    36 D3
Whelpton Clo. LN9    36 F4
Willow Clo. LN9    36 C1
Winceby Gdns. LN9    36 C3
Woodcock La. LN9    36 C3
Woodhall Rd. LN9    36 B4

## IMMINGHAM

Ainsworth Rd. DN40    37 B2
Aire Clo. DN40    37 B3
Alden Clo. DN40    37 C2
Alderney Way. DN40    37 C2
Allerton Dri. DN40    37 C2
Ancholme Av. DN40    37 A3
Anglesey Dri. DN40    37 C4
Arran Clo. DN40    37 D4
Ash Tree Clo. DN40    37 C1
Atwood Clo. DN40    37 B1
Balfour Pl. DN40    37 B2
Barnard Wk. DN40    37 D3
Battery St. DN40    37 D2
Beechwood Av. DN40    37 C2
Berwick Ct. DN40    37 D2
Birkdale Dri. DN40    37 D1
Blair Wk. DN40    37 E3
Blossom Way. DN40    37 B3
Bluestone La. DN40    37 B2
Bowman Way. DN40    37 B3
Bradford Rd. DN40    37 B2
Brewster Av. DN40    37 D3
Calder Clo. DN40    37 A3
Carver Rd. DN40    37 D3
Cedar Dri. DN40    37 C1
Chestnut Av. DN40    37 E1
Chilton Clo. DN40    37 B2
Church La. DN40    37 B1
Clarence Clo. DN40    37 B3
Cleveland Clo. DN40    37 A2
Clyfton Cres. DN40    37 B2
Collier Rd. DN40    37 D3
Copse Clo. DN40    37 C1
Corfe Clo. DN40    37 E3
Craik Hill Av. DN40    37 C3
Cushman Cres. DN40    37 C3
Deane Rd. DN40    37 D2
Dunster Wk. DN40    37 E3
Eaton Rd. DN40    37 D2
Fairisle Rise. DN40    37 D4
Ferndown Dri. DN40    37 D1
Green La. DN40    37 C3
Guernsey Gro. DN40    37 C4
Habrough Rd. DN40    37 A3
Hadleigh Rd. DN40    37 D3
Hall Park Rd. DN40    37 D1
Hamish Wk. DN40    37 B3

Hillside App. LN2 41 F6
Hillside Av. LN2 41 F6
Holdenby Clo. LN2 41 H2
Holdenby Rd. LN1 41 H2
Holmes Rd. LN1 40 B6
Honington App. LN1 40 B2
Honington Cres. LN1 40 A2
Horton St. LN1 41 E6
Howard St. LN1 40 A5
Hungate. LN1 40 C6
Hurstwood Clo. LN2 41 F1
INDUSTRIAL & RETAIL:
  Allenby Rd Ind Est.
    LN3 41 G5
  Newport Business Pk.
    LN2 41 F4
  Outercircle Ind Est.
    LN2 41 F4
Ingleby Cres. LN2 40 C1
Ironstone Clo2 41 F4
James St. LN2 40 C5
Jellicoe Av. LN2 41 G6
John St. LN2 40 D6
Keats Clo. LN2 41 F2
Keddington Av. LN1 40 C1
Kenneth St. LN1 40 C3
Kent St. LN2 41 F6
Kipling Clo. LN2 41 E2
Kingsley St. LN1 40 B4
Laceby St. LN1 41 E6
Lamb Gdns. LN2 41 E3
Laney Clo. LN2 41 F2
Langton Clo. LN2 41 E2
Langworth Gate. LN2 40 D5
Larkspur Rd. LN2 41 G2
Laughton Cres. LN2 41 E1
Laughton Way. LN2 40 C1
Laughton Way Nth.
  LN2 40 C1
Lawn Ct. LN1 40 B5
Lee Rd. LN2 40 D4
Legbourne Clo. LN1 40 B2
Lenton Grn. LN2 41 E2
Lilford Clo. LN2 41 H2
Lilford Rd. LN2 41 G2
*Lillicrap Ct,
  Chapel La. LN1 40 C5
Lillys Rd. LN1 40 C4
Lime Kiln Way. LN2 41 F5
Limelands. LN2 40 D5
Lincoln By-Pass. LN1 40 A1
Lindum Av. LN2 40 D6
Lindum Rd. LN2 40 C6
Lindum Ter. LN2 40 D5
Lissington Clo. LN2 40 C2
Long Leys Rd. LN1 40 A4
Longdales Rd. LN2 40 C3
Lucy Tower St. LN1 40 B6
Lupin Rd. LN2 41 F2
Macaulay Dri. LN2 41 E3
Mainwaring Rd. LN2 40 D4
Manor Clo. LN2 40 D4
Manor Rd. LN2 40 D4
Manton Rd. LN2 40 C3
Marigold Clo. LN2 40 D5
Marlborough Clo. LN2 41 F1
Marlowe Dri. LN2 41 E3
Marne Gdns. LN1 40 B3
Massey Rd. LN2 40 D4
May Cres. LN1 40 B5
McInnes St. LN2 41 F6
Michaelgate. LN1 40 C6
Middle St. LN1 40 A1
Middletons Fld. LN2 40 C4
Midville Clo. LN1 40 B2
Mildmay St. LN1 40 C4
Mill Rd. LN1 40 B4
Mill Row. LN1 40 B4
Millbeck Dri. LN2 41 E1
Milman Rd. LN2 41 E6
Minster Yd. LN2 40 C5
Mint La. LN1 40 C6
Mint St. LN1 40 C6
Minting Clo. LN2 40 B2
*Monks Ley Ter,
  Arboretum Av. LN2 40 D6
*Monks Manor Clo, Monks
  Manor Dri. LN2 41 E5
Monks Manor Dri. LN2 41 E5
Monks Rd. LN2 40 C6
Monks Way. LN2 41 F6
Mons Rd. LN1 40 B3
Montague St. LN2 40 D6
*Montague Ter,
  Montague St. LN2 40 D6
Montaigne Clo. LN2 41 G2

Montaigne Cres. LN2 41 G3
Montaigne Gdn. LN2 41 G2
Moor St. LN1 40 A5
Moorby Clo. LN1 40 C2
Motherby Hill. LN1 40 B6
Motherby La. LN1 40 C6
Mount St. LN1 40 B4
Naam Gro. LN1 40 B4
Naam Pl. LN1 40 B4
Napier St. LN2 41 E6
Neile Clo. LN2 41 G3
Nelson St. LN1 40 A6
Nene Rd. LN1 40 B1
Nettleham Clo. LN2 40 D3
Nettleham Rd. LN2 40 D5
Newland. LN2 40 B6
Newland St West. LN1 40 A5
Newport. LN1 40 C4
*Newport Ct,
  Newport. LN1 40 C4
Nocton Dri. LN2 40 C1
Norfolk St. LN1 40 A5
North Par. LN1 40 B5
Northgate. LN2 40 C5
*Nottingham Ter,
  Vine St. LN2 40 D6
Nursery Gro. LN2 40 D3
Oakfield St. LN2 41 E6
Oakland Clo. LN1 40 B2
Occupation Rd. LN1 40 B4
Ockbrook Clo. LN1 40 C4
Olive St. LN1 40 B4
Ongland Wk. LN2 41 G2
Orchard Rd. LN2 40 B6
Osborne Clo. LN1 40 C3
Outer Circle Dri. LN2 41 E2
Outer Circle Grn. LN2 41 F3
Outer Circle Rd. LN2 41 F3
Oval App. LN2 41 E2
Oxen Park Clo. LN2 40 D1
Park St. LN1 40 B4
Pennycress Cres. LN2 41 F2
Percy St. LN2 41 E6
Pietermaritz St. LN1 40 B1
Pine Clo. LN1 40 C1
Pottergate. LN2 40 C6
Princess Royal Clo. LN2 40 D5
Proctors Rd. LN2 41 G4
Queen Cres. LN1 40 B5
Queen Elizabeth Rd.
  LN1 40 A2
Queen Mary Rd. LN1 40 A2
Queensway. LN2 41 E5
Rasen La. LN1 40 B4
Rauceby Ter. LN1 40 B6
Ravendale Dri. LN2 40 D2
Redbourne Dri. LN2 40 D1
Remigius Gro. LN2 41 F3
Reservoir St. LN1 40 C5
Retief Clo. LN2 40 A1
Richmond Rd. LN1 40 A5
Riseholme Rd. LN1 40 C1
Riverton Clo. LN1 40 B4
Robert Tressell Wk. LN2 41 F2
Rolleston Clo. LN2 40 C2
Roman Pavement. LN2 41 F5
Roman Wharf. LN1 40 A6
Rosebery Av. LN1 40 A5
Rosemary La. LN2 40 D6
Rothwell Rd. LN2 40 C3
Roughton Clo. LN2 40 D1
Ruckland Av. LN1 40 B2
Rudgard La. LN1 40 B6
Ruskin Av. LN1 41 E3
Ruskin Grn. LN2 41 E4
Rusland Clo. LN2 40 D1
*Russell Ct,
  Cecil St. LN1 40 C4
St Annes Clo. LN2 41 E5
St Annes Rd. LN2 41 E5
St Clements Clo. LN1 41 C5
St Faiths St. LN1 40 B6
St Giles Av. LN2 40 D4
St Hugh St. LN2 40 D6
St Johns Rd. LN1 40 C4
*St Martins La,
  St Martins St. LN2 40 C6
St Martins St. LN2 40 C6
St Nicholas St. LN2 40 C6
St Pauls La. LN1 40 C5
St Rumbolds St. LN2 40 C6
*St Swithins Sq,
  Saltergate. LN2 40 C6
Saltergate. LN2 40 C6
Sanders Clo. LN2 40 A1
Saxon St. LN1 40 C4

Scopwick Pl. LN2 40 C1
Scott Gdns. LN2 41 F3
Searby Rd. LN2 41 E1
Sedgebrook Clo. LN2 40 C1
Severn St. LN1 40 A6
Sewell Rd. LN2 40 D5
Shelley Dri. LN2 41 E3
Sherbrooke St. LN2 41 G6
Sheridan Clo. LN1 41 F2
Silver St. LN2 40 C6
South Par. LN1 40 B5
Spa Bldgs. LN2 40 D6
Spa Rd. LN2 41 E6
Spa St. LN2 41 E6
Sparrow La. LN2 40 D6
Spital St. LN1 40 C4
Spring Hill. LN1 40 C4
Springfield Clo. LN1 40 C4
Stainton Gdns. LN1 40 B2
Stapleford Av. LN2 40 C1
Staunton St. LN1 40 A6
Steep Hill. LN2 40 C6
Steeping Ct. LN1 40 B2
Stonefield Av. LN2 40 C4
Strait. LN2 40 C6
Sturton Clo. LN2 40 D2
Sudbrooke Dri. LN2 40 D2
Swaby Clo. LN2 40 D1
Swan St. LN2 40 C6
Swayne Clo. LN2 41 G2
Swift Gdns. LN2 41 E2
Swift Grn. LN2 41 E2
Sympson Clo. LN2 41 G3
Tempest St. LN2 41 E6
*Temple Gdns,
  Lindum Rd. LN2 40 C6
Tennyson St. LN1 40 A5
Tetney Clo. LN1 40 C1
The Avenue. LN1 40 B6
The Grove. LN2 40 D4
The Oval. LN2 41 E2
Theodore St. LN1 40 B5
Thistle Clo. LN2 41 F1
Thomas St. LN2 40 D6
Thonock Clo. LN2 40 C3
Thoresway Dri. LN2 40 D2
Thorpe Av. LN1 40 A2
Thurlby Cres. LN1 41 E1
Thurlow St. LN2 41 G2
Tobruk Clo. LN1 40 B2
Toronto St. LN1 41 F6
Torrington Rd. LN2 40 C1
Tower Av. LN2 41 G5
Tower Cres. LN2 41 G5
Tower Dri. LN2 41 G5
Tower Gdns. LN2 41 G5
Trelawney Cres. LN1 40 B1
Troutbeck Clo. LN2 41 E1
Turner St. LN1 40 B4
Union Rd. LN1 40 B5
Unity Sq. LN2 40 C6
Upper Lindum St. LN2 40 D5
Upper Long Leys Rd.
  LN1 40 B4
Upper Saxon St. LN1 40 C4
Verdun Clo. LN1 40 B2
Vere St. LN1 40 C5
Vicars Ct. LN1 40 C5
Victoria Pass. LN1 40 B5
Victoria St. LN1 40 B6
Victoria Ter. LN1 40 B5
Vine St. LN2 40 D6
Waddingworth Gro.
  LN2 40 D1
Wake St. LN1 40 B4
Waldeck St. LN1 40 B4
Walmer St. LN2 41 F6
Waterside Nth. LN2 40 C6
Wavell Dri. LN3 41 G6
Wavell Rd. LN3 41 G6
*Welbeck St,
  Ashfield St. LN2 41 E6
Welbourn Gdns. LN2 40 D1
Well La. LN2 40 C6
Welland Rd. LN1 40 A2
Wellingore Rd. LN2 40 D1
Wellington St. LN1 40 A5
Welton Gdns. LN2 40 C1
West Par. LN1 40 A5
Westbourne Gro. LN1 40 B6
Westcliffe St. LN1 40 B3
Westfield St. LN1 40 A5
Westgate. LN1 40 C5
Westholm Clo. LN2 40 B6
Whitehall Gro. LN1 40 B6
Wickenby Cres. LN1 40 B2

Wigford Way. LN1 40 B6
Williamson St. LN1 40 C4
Willingham Av. LN2 40 C2
Willis Clo. LN1 40 B5
Wilson St. LN1 40 B4
Windermere Rd. LN2 41 F1
Windmill Vw. LN1 40 B4
Wingrave St. LN1 40 B3
Winn St. LN2 40 D6
Winniffe Gdns. LN2 41 G2
Winnowsty La. LN2 40 D6
Winster Clo. LN2 40 D1
Woburn Av. LN1 40 C3
Woodburn Clo. LN1 40 C1
Woodhall Dri. LN2 40 C1
Woodrush Rd. LN2 41 F1
Woodstock St. LN1 40 A5
*Wordsworth St,
  Drury La. LN1 40 C5
Wragby Rd. LN2 40 D5
Wrightsway. LN2 41 G4
Yarborough Cres. LN1 40 B3
Yarborough Rd. LN1 40 B5
Yarborough Ter. LN1 40 B5
Yates Clo. LN1 40 A5
York Av. LN1 40 A5

## LOUTH

Abbey Rd. LN11 45 G3
Abbotts Way. LN11 45 H3
Ada Way. LN11 45 G2
Adrian Clo. LN11 45 F5
Albany Pl. LN11 45 G6
Albany Rd. LN11 45 F6
Albion Pl. LN11 45 F4
Alder Clo. LN11 45 G5
Alexander Dri. LN11 45 G6
Alexandra Rd. LN11 45 F3
Almond Cres. LN11 45 G4
Althorp Gdns. LN11 44 D2
Alvingham Rd. LN11 45 H1
Amanda Dri. LN11 45 F1
Andrews Clo. LN11 45 F2
Anthony Cres. LN11 45 F1
Arundel Dri. LN11 44 D2
Ash Clo. LN11 45 F2
Ashley Rd. LN11 45 F4
Aswell St. LN11 45 E4
Badminton Way. LN11 44 D2
Bartongate. LN11 45 F6
Beck Way. LN11 45 G5
*Becketts Ct,
  Riverside Ct. LN11 45 G3
Beckside Ct. LN11 45 G6
Beech Gro. LN11 45 F2
Beeton Ct. LN11 45 F5
Belton Walk. LN11 44 D2
Belvoir Ct. LN11 45 E1
Belvoir Way. LN11 45 E1
Birch Rd. LN11 45 G4
Bishops Clo. LN11 45 H3
Blanchard Rd. LN11 45 G5
Blenheim Clo. LN11 45 E2
Bluestone Rise. LN11 45 E5
Bowers Av. LN11 45 F2
Bracken Way. LN11 45 F3
Brackenborough Rd.
  LN11 45 F1
Bradley Clo. LN11 45 G6
Bramley Clo. LN11 45 F4
Breakneck la. LN11 44 D4
Bridge St. LN11 45 E3
Bridle Clo. LN11 45 F3
Broadbank. LN11 45 E3
Broadley Cres. LN11 45 G3
Brookside Rd. LN11 45 F6
Buckingham Rd. LN11 44 D2
Burghley Cres. LN11 45 E2
*Burnt Hill Clo,
  Eastgate. LN11 45 E4
Burton Ct. LN11 45 G5
Cannon St. LN11 45 E4
Castle Way. LN11 44 D1
Cedar Clo. LN11 45 F2
Charles Av. LN11 45 G2
Charles St. LN11 45 E4
Chatsworth Dri. LN11 45 E2
Chequergate. LN11 45 E4
Chestnut Dri. LN11 45 H3
Chrisopher Clo. LN11 45 E4
Church Clo. LN11 45 E4
Church St. LN11 45 H1

Church St. LN11 45 F4
Cinder La. LN11 45 E4
Cisterngate. LN11 45 E3
Commercial Rd. LN11 45 G3
Cordeaux Clo. LN11 45 F2
Corn Mkt. LN11 45 E4
Coronation Clo. LN11 45 F2
Cowslip La. LN11 45 H1
Crown Wk. LN11 45 G4
Crowtree La. LN11 44 C5
Cuppleditch Way. LN11 45 F2
David Av. LN11 45 G2
Dove Clo. LN11 45 F2
Eastfield Ct. LN11 45 G3
Eastfield Rise. LN11 45 F2
Eastfield Rd. LN11 45 F3
Eastgate. LN11 45 E4
Edward St. LN11 45 E4
*Elizabeth Ct,
  Church St. LN11 45 F4
Elkington Rd. LN11 44 C4
Elm Dri. LN11 45 G2
Eresbie Rd. LN11 45 G6
Eve St. LN11 45 E3
Fairfield Ind Est. LN11 45 E1
Fanthorpe La. LN11 44 C1
Florence Wright Av.
  LN11 45 G6
Fowler Clo. LN11 45 G5
Freer Gdns. LN11 45 H4
Fulmar Clo. LN11 45 F1
George St. LN11 45 E4
Glamis Pl. LN11 45 E3
Goodwood Clo. LN11 44 D2
Gospelgate. LN11 45 E4
Graye Dri. LN11 45 G6
Grays Ct. LN11 45 E3
*Grays Rd,
  Cisterngate. LN11 45 E4
Gresley Rd. LN11 45 F5
Grimsby Rd. LN11 44 D1
Grosvenor Cres. LN11 45 G2
Grosvenor Rd. LN11 45 F2
Hardwick Clo. LN11 44 D2
Harewood Cres. LN11 45 E2
Havelock Clo. LN11 45 G5
Hawker Dri. LN11 45 G5
Hawksmede Way. LN11 45 F1
Hawthorne Av. LN11 45 E3
Hazel Gro. LN11 45 G5
High Holme Rd. LN11 45 E3
Hill Rise Clo. LN11 44 D2
Hill Ter. LN11 45 F5
Holmes Clo. LN11 45 F2
Horncastle La. LN11 44 C6
Hunter Pl. LN11 45 E5
INDUSTRIAL & RETAIL:
  Fairfield Ind Est. LN11 45 E1
  Irish Hill. LN11 44 D4
  James St. LN11 45 E3
  Jenkins Clo. LN11 45 F1
  Jubilee Cres. LN11 45 F2
  Keddington Cres. LN11 45 F2
  Keddington Rd. LN11 45 F2
Kenwick Clo. LN11 45 G6
Kenwick Gdns. LN11 45 G6
Kenwick Pastures. LN11 45 G6
Kenwick Rd. LN11 45 G6
Kestrel Dri. LN11 45 F1
Kidgate. LN11 45 E4
*Kiln La,
  Broadbank. LN11 45 E3
Kings Ct. LN11 45 H2
Laburnum Cres. LN11 45 G3
Lacey Gdns. LN11 45 G3
Langley Clo. LN11 45 F2
Leakes Row. LN11 45 F2
Lee St. LN11 45 E4
Legbourne Rd. LN11 45 G6
*Library Clo,
  Northgate. LN11 45 E4
Lime Gro. LN11 45 E5
Linda Cres. LN11 45 E5
Linden Wk. LN11 45 G5
Lindsey Way. LN11 45 G5
*Little Eastgate Clo,
  Upgate. LN11 45 E4
Little La. LN11 45 F4
Little South St. LN11 45 E4
Lock Keepers Way.
  LN11 45 G2
London Rd. LN11 45 E5
Longleat Dri. LN11 44 D2
Love La. LN11 44 D4
Lucern Clo. LN11 45 G2
*Lucern Ct,
  Thames Rd. LN11 45 G3

Luda Ter. LN11 45 G2
Lyndon Cres. LN11 45 G1
Lyndon Way. LN11 45 G1
Maple Clo. LN11 45 F2
Market Pl. LN11 45 E4
Martin Clo. LN11 45 F1
Mayfield Cres. LN11 45 G5
Meadow Clo. LN11 45 F5
Mercer Row. LN11 45 E4
Meridian Vw. LN11 45 E5
Mill La. LN11 45 E3
Mill La. LN11 45 E6
Millers Ct. LN11 45 E3
Millgood Clo. LN11 45 G4
Minster Dri. LN11 45 G5
Monks Av. LN11 45 F4
Monks Dyke Head. LN11 45 F4
Monks Dyke Rd. LN11 45 F4
Mount Olivet. LN11 45 E3
Mount Pleasant. LN11 45 F4
New St. LN11 45 E4
Newbridge Hill. LN11 45 F3
Newmarket. LN11 45 E4
*Nichol Hill, Eastgate. LN11 45 E4
*North Holme Ct, North Holme Rd. LN11 45 F2
North Holme Rd. LN11 44 D2
Northgate. LN11 45 E4
*Northgate Pl, Northgate. LN11 45 E4
Oak Clo. LN11 45 G5
Oak Ct. LN11 45 G5
Old Mill Pk. LN11 45 F2
Orchard Clo. LN11 45 F2
Orme La. LN11 45 G3
Park Av. LN11 45 H2
Park Row. LN11 45 H2
Parsons Halt. LN11 45 F4
Pasture Dri. LN11 45 F4
Pawn Shop Pass. LN11 45 E4
Pippin Clo. LN11 45 F4
Pleasant Pl. LN11 45 F4
Priory Clo. LN11 45 F4
Priory Rd. LN11 45 F4
Pulman Ter. LN11 45 F3
Quarry Rd. LN11 45 E5
Quarryside. LN11 45 E5
Queen St. LN11 45 G5
Queens Way. LN11 45 G4
Queens Ct. LN11 45 G5
Quorn Gdns. LN11 45 G5
Ramsgate. LN11 45 F3
Ramsgate Rd. LN11 45 F3
River La. LN11 45 H2
Riverhead Rd. LN11 45 G3
Riverhead Ter. LN11 45 G3
Riverside Ct. LN11 45 G3
Robinson La. LN11 45 F5
Rookery Clo. LN11 45 G2
*Royal Oak Ct, Upgate. LN11 45 E4
Russet Dri. LN11 45 F5
St Bernards Av. LN11 45 G3
St Bernards Clo. LN11 45 G3
St James Vw. LN11 45 E5
St Marys La. LN11 44 D4
St Marys Pk. LN11 44 D3
St Michaels Rd. LN11 45 F5
Sandringham Dri. LN11 45 E2
School Ho La. LN11 45 E4
Seymour Av. LN11 45 F5
Shearwater Clo. LN11 45 F1
Sherwood Clo. LN11 45 G6
Simons Clo. LN11 45 G6
South Ter. LN11 45 F5
Southfield Dri. LN11 45 F5
Southlands Av. LN11 45 G6
Spaw La. LN11 45 E3
Spire View Rd. LN11 45 G4
Spital Hill. LN11 45 E5
Spout Yd. LN11 45 E4
Spring Ct. LN11 45 F4
Spring Gdns. LN11 45 E4
Stainesway. LN11 45 G2
Station App. LN11 45 F3
Stewton Gdns. LN11 45 G5
Stewton La. LN11 45 F5
Stutte Clo. LN11 45 G5
Sudbury Pl. LN11 45 E5
Swallow Dri. LN11 45 F1
Sycamore Dri. LN11 45 G5
Tattershall Way. LN11 44 D1
Temple Ter. LN11 45 F5
Tennyson Rd. LN11 45 F5

Thames St. LN11 45 G3
The Crescent. LN11 45 E3
The Link. LN11 45 H4
The Moorings. LN11 45 G2
The Sidings. LN11 45 F3
Thorpe La. LN11 44 D4
Ticklepenny Wk. LN11 45 G2
Trinity La. LN11 45 F3
Tudor Dri. LN11 45 F5
Union St. LN11 45 E3
Upgate. LN11 45 E4
Vanessa Rd. LN11 44 D5
Vickers La. LN11 45 F2
Victoria Rd. LN11 45 F2
Virginia Dri. LN11 45 H4
Wallis Rd. LN11 45 G4
Warwick Rd. LN11 45 E1
Watts La. LN11 45 F5
*Wellington Mews, Wellington St. LN11 45 F3
Wellington St. LN11 45 F3
Westgate. LN11 44 D4
Willow Dri. LN11 45 F1
Windsor Mews. LN11 45 F4
Windsor Rd. LN11 45 E2
Woburn Clo. LN11 45 G5
Wood La. LN11 45 G5
Wood Way. LN11 45 H4
Woodlands. LN11 45 F3
Woodvale Rise. LN11 44 D3
Worcester Clo. LN11 45 F5

## MABLETHORPE

Admiralty Rd. LN12 46 C2
Alexandra Pk. LN12 46 B3
Alexandra Rd. LN12 46 B2
Alford Rd. LN12 46 A3
Ancaster Rd. LN12 46 C3
Aqua Dri. LN12 46 B4
Arden Clo. LN12 46 C5
Berkeley Ct. LN12 46 B3
Brooke Dri. LN12 46 C4
Byron Clo. LN12 46 B1
Byron Rd. LN12 46 B1
Champion Way. LN12 46 C5
Chaucer Av. LN12 46 B2
Cheltenham Way. LN12 46 A4
Church La. LN12 46 A3
Church Rd. LN12 46 A3
Dymoke Clo. LN12 46 C4
Dymoke Rd. LN12 46 C4
Eagle Clo. LN12 46 A2
Elm Av. LN12 46 C4
Enterprise Rd. LN12 46 A1
Eton Rd. LN12 46 D6
Fitzwilliam St. LN12 46 B2
Foxe End. LN12 46 C3
George St. LN12 46 C3
Gibraltar Rd. LN12 46 C2
Golf Rd. LN12 46 A1
Grift Bank. LN12 46 C4
Grosvenor Ct. LN12 46 B3
Grosvenor Rd. LN12 46 B3
Hamilton Rd. LN12 46 A2
Hammond Ct. LN12 46 B3
Harlequin Dri. LN12 46 C4
Harris Blvd. LN12 46 C4
Harrow Rd. LN12 46 B2
High St. LN12 46 A3
Ivel Clo. LN12 46 A1
Ivel Gro. LN12 46 B1
Jacklin Cres. LN12 46 A1
James Av. LN12 46 D6
Kensington Gdns. LN12 46 C4
King St. LN12 46 C4
Kingsley Rd. LN12 46 A2
Knowle La. LN12 46 B3
Locksley Rd. LN12 46 C4
Long Acre. LN12 46 B1
Lyle Clo. LN12 46 A1
Main St. LN12 46 C6
Malvern Rd. LN12 46 B2
Marian Av. LN12 46 C4
Marian Av. LN12 46 C5
Marina Rd. LN12 46 C4
Marlborough Dri. LN12 46 A3
Marlow Dri. LN12 46 B3
Maxwell Dri. LN12 46 B3
Mayflower Way. LN12 46 B3
Medina Gdns. LN12 46 C5
Mill Field. LN12 46 D5
Nelson Rd. LN12 46 B3
Newstead Rd. LN12 46 C4

North Rd. LN12 46 B6
Oakham Av. LN12 46 A4
Ocean Ct. LN12 46 D4
Orchard Clo. LN12 46 A3
Orchard Way. LN12 46 A3
Park Av. LN12 46 C3
Parklands. LN12 46 A3
Parry Rd. LN12 46 C3
Phoenix Clo. LN12 46 B3
Promenade. LN12 46 C2
Quebec Rd. LN12 46 B1
Queens Park Clo. LN12 46 C4
Queensway. LN12 46 B2
Regent Rd. LN12 46 A1
Repton Rd. LN12 46 B2
Ripon Pl. LN12 46 C3
Rugby Rd. LN12 46 B2
Ruskin Rd. LN12 46 B2
Rutland Rd. LN12 46 A3
St Andrews Rd. LN12 46 B1
St Peters La. LN12 46 D6
Seacroft Rd. LN12 46 B2
Seaholme Rd. LN12 46 A5
Sherwood Rd. LN12 46 B2
Somersby Av. LN12 46 B2
Stanley Av. LN12 46 B3
Station Rd. LN12 46 B2
Strand Clo. LN12 46 B3
Sutton Rd. LN12 46 D5
Tennyson Av. LN12 46 B2
Tennyson Rd. LN12 46 B2
The Boulevard. LN12 46 C3
The Drive. LN12 46 A1
The Fairway. LN12 46 A1
The Forge. LN12 46 A3
The Green. LN12 46 A2
The Meadows. LN12 46 C6
The Strand. LN12 46 B3
Tower Clo. LN12 46 B4
Trenchard Rd. LN12 46 C3
Victoria Rd. LN12 46 C3
Vyner Clo. LN12 46 C3
Waterloo Rd. LN12 46 C5
Wellington Av. LN12 46 B2
Wellington Rd. LN12 46 B2
Whitehead Clo. LN12 46 A1
Winchester Dri. LN12 46 A4
Windsor Rd. LN12 46 B2

## MARKET DEEPING/ DEEPING ST. JAMES

Allen Clo. PE6 47 E3
Althorpe Clo. PE6 47 A3
Ascendale. PE6 47 F3
Back La. PE6 47 F4
Beaufort Av. PE6 47 C2
Beech Clo. PE6 47 B2
Bell La. PE6 47 E4
Belton Clo. PE6 47 A3
Belvoir Clo. PE6 47 A2
Black Prince Av. PE6 47 B2
Blackthorn Clo. PE6 47 D2
Bluebells. PE6 47 D2
Bramley Rd. PE6 47 D4
Bridge St. PE6 47 F3
Broadgate La. PE6 47 E4
Brownlow Dri. PE6 47 E4
Bryony Way. PE6 47 D2
Burchnall Clo. PE6 47 D2
Burghley Clo. PE6 47 F4
Burnside Av. PE6 47 A2
Buttercup Ct. PE6 47 D2
Campion Clo. PE6 47 D2
Cedar Clo. PE6 47 B3
Chatsworth Clo. PE6 47 A3
Cherry Gro. PE6 47 C3
Chestnut Way. PE6 47 B2
Church St, Deeping St. James. PE6 47 E4
Church St, Market Deeping. PE6 47 E4
Clover Clo. PE6 47 C3
Courtfields. PE6 47 C1
Cowslip Dri. PE6 47 D2
Cromwell Way. PE6 47 A2
Crowfields. PE6 47 F3
Crowson Way. PE6 47 D3
Curlew Walk. PE6 47 D3
Deene Clo. PE6 47 A3
Deeping St James Rd. PE6 47 E4
Dixons Rd. PE6 47 C3

Douglas Rd. PE6 47 C3
Dovecote Rd. PE6 47 B2
Eastfield. PE6 47 C2
Eastgate. PE6 47 F4
Elm Clo. PE6 47 D3
Ermine Way. PE6 47 F3
Exeter Clo. PE6 47 E3
Fairfax Way. PE6 47 E4
Feneley Clo. PE6 47 C2
Florence Way. PE6 47 C2
Forge Ct. PE6 47 B2
Foxgloves. PE6 47 D2
Fraser Clo. PE6 47 D3
Glebe Vw. PE6 47 B2
Godsey Cres. PE6 47 C3
Godseys La. PE6 47 B2
Green Walk. PE6 47 A3
Grimsthorpe Clo. PE6 47 A2
Halfleet. PE6 47 A2
Hall Farm. PE6 47 B2
Hall Meadow Rd. PE6 47 F1
Hawthorn Clo. PE6 47 E4
Hereward Way. PE6 47 E4
High St. PE6 47 B3
Holland Clo. PE6 47 A2
Holly Way. PE6 47 E3
Horsegate. PE6 47 D4
John Wake Clo. PE6 47 B2
John Eve Way. PE6 47 B2
Kesteven Dri. PE6 47 A2
Knight Clo. PE6 47 D3
Lady Margarets Av. PE6 47 C2
Lamport Clo. PE6 47 A2
Lancaster Way. PE6 47 B1
Lark Rise. PE6 47 C2
Lime Tree Av. PE6 47 A2
Linchfield Clo. PE6 47 E3
Linchfield Rd. PE6 47 D1
Lincoln Clo. PE6 47 A2
Lincoln Rd. PE6 47 B3
Lindsey Av. PE6 47 A2
Linnet Clo. PE6 47 D3
Manor Way. PE6 47 E4
Marigolds. PE6 47 D2
Market Deeping By-Pass. PE6 47 A1
Maxey Clo. PE6 47 A3
Meadow Rd. PE6 47 C2
Meadway. PE6 47 A2
Millfield La. PE6 47 A2
Millfield Rd. PE6 47 E4
New Row. PE6 47 D4
Nightingales. PE6 47 C3
North Field Rd. PE6 47 A1
Osbourne Way. PE6 47 D4
Panton Clo. PE6 47 D3
Park Dri. PE6 47 B3
Park Estate. PE6 47 E4
Park Rd. PE6 47 D4
Pawlett Clo. PE6 47 D3
Peakirk Rd. PE6 47 E4
Pendlebury Dri. PE6 47 D3
Peterborough Rd. PE6 47 A1
Petworth Clo. PE6 47 A2
Prestland. PE6 47 B2
Primroses. PE6 47 D2
Priory Clo. PE6 47 F4
Queens Av. PE6 47 C2
Riverside. PE6 47 F4
Robin Clo. PE6 47 C3
Rockingham Clo. PE6 47 A2
Rosemary Av. PE6 47 D2
Rycroft Av. PE6 47 F3
Rycroft Clo. PE6 47 F3
St Guthlac Av. PE6 47 B2
St James Mews. PE6 47 D4
Sandringham Way. PE6 47 A2
Sewell Clo. PE6 47 E3
Shackleton Clo. PE6 47 B1
Spalding Rd. PE6 47 F4
Speedwell Ct. PE6 47 D2
Stamford Clo. PE6 47 B3
Stamford Rd. PE6 47 A3
Still Clo. PE6 47 B3
Stirling Way. PE6 47 C1
Suttons La. PE6 47 C4
Swallow Walk. PE6 47 D3
Sweet Clo. PE6 47 D3
Swift Clo. PE6 47 D3
Tattershall Dri. PE6 47 D2
Teasles. PE6 47 D2
Thackers Way. PE6 47 C3
The Acorns. PE6 47 B1
The Avenue. PE6 47 B3
The Brambles. PE6 47 D2

The Grove. PE6 47 B3
The Lees. PE6 47 E3
The Meadows. PE6 47 C2
The Spinney. PE6 47 B2
The Orchard. PE6 47 B3
The Paddock. PE6 47 A2
The Parslins. PE6 47 F3
The Pasture. PE6 47 C2
The Woodlands. PE6 47 B3
Thyme Av. PE6 47 C3
Towngate East. PE6 47 A2
Towngate West. PE6 47 A2
Towning Clo. PE6 47 D2
Tudor Pl. PE6 47 F3
Tyghes Clo. PE6 47 B3
Wade Park Av. PE6 47 C3
Waterton Clo. PE6 47 E4
Welland Way. PE6 47 E4
Wellington Way. PE6 47 B1
Whitley Way. PE6 47 C1
Willoughby Av. PE6 47 C2
Woburn Clo. PE6 47 A2
Woodcroft Clo. PE6 47 A3
Wren Clo. PE6 47 C3

## MARKET RASEN/ MIDDLE RASEN

Anglian Way. LN8 48 F3
Ashtree Wall. LN8 48 D4
Beechers Way. LN8 48 E4
Braemar Av. LN8 48 A2
Caistor Rd. LN8 48 E1
Cedar Clo. LN8 48 E3
Chapel St. LN8 48 E3
Chapman St. LN8 48 F3
Charlotte Clo. LN8 48 F2
Church St, Market Rasen. LN8 48 E2
Church St, Middle Rasen. LN8 48 A2
Churchill Av. LN8 48 D3
Coronation Rd. LN8 48 D2
Dear St. LN8 48 D2
Dovecote. LN8 48 A2
Farriers Way. LN8 48 F4
Gainsborough Rd. LN8 48 A3
Gallamore Ct. LN8 48 B2
Gallamore La. LN8 48 B2
George St. LN8 48 E2
Gordon Field. LN8 48 E4
Green La. LN8 48 D3
Holly Tree Clo. LN8 48 D3
Horseshoe Way. LN8 48 F3
Jameson Bridge St. LN8 48 E2
John St. LN8 48 E3
Kilnwell Rd. LN8 48 E3
King St. LN8 48 D2
Lady Francis Dri. LN8 48 E2
Lammas Leas Rd. LN8 48 E3
Legsby Rd. LN8 48 F3
Linwood Rd. LN8 48 E2
Low Church Rd. LN8 48 B2
Low La. LN8 48 B1
Market Pl. LN8 48 E2
Mayfield Cres. LN8 48 B2
Meadowfield. LN8 48 B2
Mill La. LN8 48 B4
Mill Rd. LN8 48 D4
Mill St. LN8 48 E2
Naylors Dri. LN8 48 A2
North St. LN8 48 A2
Nursery St. LN8 48 E3
Oak Tree Clo. LN8 48 E3
Orchard Way. LN8 48 F2
Oxford St. LN8 48 E3
Pasture La. LN8 48 F3
Queen St. LN8 48 E3
Rase La. LN8 48 E2
Saddlers Way. LN8 48 F4
St Peters Clo. LN8 48 A2
Serpentine St. LN8 48 E3
Stable Way. LN8 48 F4
The Maltings Ct. LN8 48 A2
The Orchards. LN8 48 A2
The Poplars. LN8 48 F3
The Ridings. LN8 48 F3
Union St. LN8 48 E3
Velden Way. LN8 48 D3
Victoria Rd. LN8 48 F2
Walesby Rd. LN8 48 F1
Waterloo St. LN8 48 E2
Wellesley Clo. LN8 48 E2

Wells Dri. LN8 48 F4
Wetherby Clo. LN8 48 F4
Whitworth Way. LN8 48 F4
Wilkinson Dri. LN8 48 A3
Willingham Rd. LN8 48 E3

## METHERINGHAM

Alexander Clo. LN4 34 D5
Alfred Av. LN4 34 B5
Apple Tree Clo. LN4 34 B5
Ashdale Clo. LN4 34 A5
Barley Clo. LN4 34 B5
Bentley Way. LN4 34 A5
Blacksmith Clo. LN4 34 B4
Blankney Rd. LN4 34 C6
Caroline Rd. LN4 34 C5
Cavalry Ct. LN4 34 C4
Chaplin Clo. LN4 34 A5
Cherrytree Way. LN4 34 A5
Chestnut Clo. LN4 34 B4
Church La. LN4 34 C5
Church Wk. LN4 34 C5
Dane Clo. LN4 34 B6
De Wint Clo. LN4 34 B4
Drury St. LN4 34 C5
Dunston Rd. LN4 34 B4
Farrier Ct. LN4 34 C4
Fen Rd. LN4 34 C5
Field Farm La. LN4 34 C5
Flinders Clo. LN4 34 B4
Flintham Clo. LN4 34 A5
Franklin Clo. LN4 34 B4
Granary Clo. LN4 34 A5
Grange Rd. LN4 34 C5
Hall Yard. LN4 34 B5
Harvest Clo. LN4 34 B5
High St. LN4 34 B5
Highfields Rise. LN4 34 B6
Hunters Dri. LN4 34 B4
Kings Rd. LN4 34 A5
Lime Tree Av. LN4 34 C5
Lincoln Rd. LN4 34 A5
Londesborough Way.
LN4 34 C5
Manor Clo. LN4 34 D5
Manor Rd. LN4 34 C6
Meadow Clo. LN4 34 C5
Metheringham Fen La.
LN4 34 C5
Metheringham Heath La.
LN4 34 A5
Middle St. LN4 34 C5
Millfield Rd. LN4 34 A5
Moor La. LN4 34 D5
Newton Clo. LN4 34 B4
Norman Cres. LN4 34 B6
Orchard Clo. LN4 34 B5
Paddock La. LN4 34 C4
Park Cres. LN4 34 D5
Princes St. LN4 34 B6
Princess Margaret Av.
LN4 34 B6
Pullman Clo. LN4 34 D5
Roman Clo. LN4 34 C5
Rossington Clo. LN4 34 B4
Rowan Way. LN4 34 B5
Saddlers Clo. LN4 34 C4
St Wilfreds Clo. LN4 34 C5
Sargent Clo. LN4 34 B4
Saxon Clo. LN4 34 C5
Shiregate. LN4 34 B4
Skipwith Cres. LN4 34 A4
Sleaford Rd. LN4 34 B5
Station Rd. LN4 34 B5
Tennyson Clo. LN4 34 B5
The Chase. LN4 34 B4
Viking Way. LN4 34 B6
Wesley Clo. LN4 34 B5
Westfield Clo. LN4 34 C5

## NETTLEHAM

Aima Ct. LN2 49 C1
All Saints La. LN2 49 B1
Ash Tree Av. LN2 49 D2
Beckside. LN2 49 B3
Beech Av. LN2 49 B3
Bramble Clo. LN2 49 D3
Bridge St. LN2 49 C2
Brookfield Av. LN2 49 D2
Chapel La. LN2 49 C2
Cherry Tree La. LN2 49 B3
Church St. LN2 49 C2
Cliff Av. LN2 49 C2
Cotton Smith Way. LN2 49 C1
Crescent Clo. LN2 49 C2
Cross St. LN2 49 C2
Dalderby Cres. LN2 49 B2
Deepdale La. LN2 49 A1
East St. LN2 49 C2
Eastway. LN2 49 D3
Field Clo. LN2 49 D3
Greenfields. LN2 49 C2
Greetwell La. LN2 49 B3
Heath Rd. LN2 49 C1
Herrington Av. LN2 49 D1
High Leas. LN2 49 D1
High St. LN2 49 B2
Highfields. LN2 49 C1
Kerrison Vw. LN2 49 D1
Kingsway. LN2 49 B2
Lacy Clo. LN2 49 D3
Larch Av. LN2 49 C2
Lincoln Rd. LN2 49 A3
Lodge La. LN2 49 D2
Manor Ct. LN2 49 B2
Mansford Clo. LN2 49 C1
Midway Clo. LN2 49 D2
Mill Hill. LN2 49 C2
North Ct. LN2 49 C2
North St. LN2 49 C2
Orchard Way. LN2 49 C2
Parkside. LN2 49 D2
Poachers Mdw. LN2 49 D2
Ridgeway. LN2 49 C2
Riseholme La. LN2 49 A2
Riverdale. LN2 49 D2
Scothern Rd. LN2 49 C1
Shaw Way. LN2 49 C1
Squires Pl. LN2 49 D2
Sudbrook La. LN2 49 D2
Sutton Clo. LN2 49 B2
The Chestnuts. LN2 49 B2
The Crescent. LN2 49 C2
The Croft. LN2 49 C3
The Dales. LN2 49 C3
The Dene. LN2 49 C1
The Green. LN2 49 C2
The Hawthorns. LN2 49 D2
The Oaks. LN2 49 D2
The Rowans. LN2 49 B2
The Steepers. LN2 49 D1
Vicarage La. LN2 49 C2
Washdyke La. LN2 49 A2
Watermill La. LN2 49 B2
Welton Rd. LN2 49 A2
Westway. LN2 49 A2
Willowfield Av. LN2 49 D2
Wold Vw. LN2 49 D1

## NEW BOULTHAM/ CANWICK

Abbot St. LN5 42 C2
Albany Ter. LN5 42 B6
Alfred St. LN5 42 B2
Altham Ter. LN5 42 A4
Anchor St. LN5 42 B2
Archer St. LN5 42 C2
Arthur St. LN5 42 D2
Ashtons Ct. LN5 42 C2
Baker St. LN5 42 B1
Bargate. LN5 42 B4
Beech St. LN5 42 B6
Beevor St. LN6 42 A1
Bell St. LN5 42 B3
Bishop Kings Ct. LN5 42 C3
Boultham Av. LN5 42 B2
Boultham Park Rd. LN6 42 A3
Boundary St. LN5 42 B5
Brancaster Dri. LN5 42 A3
Brayford St. LN5 42 C1
Brayford Way. LN5 42 B1
Brayford Wharf E. LN5 42 B1
Bristol Dri. LN6 42 A3
Canwick Av. LN5 43 E4
Canwick Hill. LN5 43 E4
Canwick Rd. LN5 42 C1
Centaur Rd. LN5 42 A1
Centurion Rd. LN5 42 B2
Chaplin St. LN5 42 C2
Charles St. LN5 42 C2
Chelmsford St. LN5 42 C2
Church Dri. LN6 42 A2
Clayton Rd. LN5 42 B5
Clifton St. LN5 42 D2
Clive Av. LN6 42 A3
Clumber St. LN5 42 B2
Colegrave St. LN5 42 B4
Coningsby Cres. LN4 42 C6
Connaught Ter. LN5 42 B6
Cornhill. LN5 42 C1
Coulson St. LN6 42 A2
Crane Gro. LN6 42 A4
Cranwell St. LN5 42 B3
*Craven Mews,
 Craven St. LN5 42 B3
Craven St. LN5 42 B3
Cross O'Cliff Clo. LN5 42 C5
Cross O'Cliff Hill. LN5 42 B4
Cross Spencer St. LN5 42 C3
Cross St. LN5 42 C3
Crusader Rd. LN6 42 A3
Dale St. LN5 43 E2
Derby St. LN5 42 B4
Dixon Clo. LN5 42 A3
Dixon St. LN5 42 A3
Dixon Way. LN5 42 B3
Dunford Clo. LN5 42 D2
Dunlop St. LN5 42 A3
Earls Dri. LN6 42 A3
Edna St. LN5 42 B3
Edward St. LN5 42 B3
Elder St. LN5 42 B6
Eleanor Clo. LN5 42 B5
Elliot Rd. LN5 42 D2
Ellison St. LN5 42 B6
Ewart St. LN5 42 B6
Fairfax St. LN5 42 B3
Featherby Pl. LN5 42 B3
Firth Rd. LN5 42 B3
Foster St. LN5 42 B2
Francis St. LN5 42 B6
Frank St. LN5 42 B3
Frank Swaby Ct. LN5 42 B5
Gaunt St. LN5 42 B2
George St. LN5 43 E2
Gibbeson St. LN5 42 B3
Glenwood Gro. LN6 42 A3
Grace St. LN5 42 C2
Grainsby Clo. LN6 42 A6
Grange Clo. LN4 43 F3
Grange La. LN4 43 E3
Great Northern Ter.
LN5 42 D1
Green La. LN6 42 A1
Gresley Dri. LN6 42 B3
Hall Dri. LN5 43 E3
Hall Dri. LN4 43 E3
Hall Gdns. LN4 43 E3
Hallam Gro. LN6 42 A4
Hamilton Rd. LN5 42 B5
Heighington Rd. LN4 43 E4
Henley St. LN5 42 C3
Henry St. LN5 42 C3
Hermit St. LN5 42 C2
High St. LN5 42 B3
Hood St. LN5 42 C2
Hope St. LN5 42 D2
INDUSTRIAL & RETAIL:
Great Northern Ind Est.
LN5 43 E1
Sunningdale Trading Est.
LN6 42 A3
Kesteven St. LN5 42 C1
King St. LN5 42 C2
Kingsway. LN5 42 D3
Kirkby St. LN5 42 C2
Knight Pl. LN5 42 C3
Knight St. LN5 42 C3
Lake View Rd. LN6 42 A6
Lancaster Pl. LN5 42 A6
Lansdowne Av. LN6 42 A6
Lewis St. LN5 42 C2
Lincoln Av. LN6 42 A4
Lincoln Rd. LN4 43 E4
Linton St. LN5 42 C3
Little Bargate St. LN5 42 C3
Lonsdale Pl. LN5 42 A3
Lorne St. LN5 42 D1
Lumley St. LN5 42 C2
Lytton St. LN5 43 E1
Manby St. LN5 42 B5
Maple St. LN5 42 B6
Marjorie Av. LN6 42 A3
Martin St. LN5 42 C2
Matilda Rd. LN6 42 A2
Mayfair Av. LN4 42 A4
Melville St. LN5 42 D1
Mill La. LN5 42 B2
Milton St. LN5 42 B5
Monson St. LN5 42 D2
Montague Rd. LN4 11 E3
Murdock Rd. LN5 42 B5
Nelthorpe St. LN5 42 B2
Newark Rd. LN5 42 A6
Newton St. LN2 42 C1
Norman St. LN5 42 C1
Norris St. LN5 42 C1
Oxford St. LN5 42 C1
Peel St. LN5 42 B3
Pelham La. LN4 43 E3
Pelham St. LN2 42 B2
Pennell St. LN5 42 B2
Peppercorn Clo. LN6 42 B6
Poplar St. LN5 42 B6
Portland St. LN5 42 B2
Princess St. LN5 42 B2
Prior St. LN5 42 C2
Queen St. LN5 42 B3
Quorn Dri. LN66 42 A4
Railway Clo. LN6 42 A2
Railway Pk Mews. LN6 42 A2
Ripon St. LN5 42 C2
Robey St. LN5 42 B3
Rookery La. LN6 42 A6
Rope Walk. LN6 42 B1
Russell St. LN5 42 B1
St Andrews Clo. PL5 42 C2
St Andrews Dri. LN6 42 A3
St Andrews Pl. LN5 42 C2
*St Botolphs Ct,
 St Botolphs Cres. LN5 42 B3
St Botolphs Cres. LN5 42 B3
St Catherines. LN5 42 B4
St Catherines Clo. LN5 42 B5
St Catherines Gro. LN5 42 B4
St Catherines Rd. LN5 42 B4
St Mark St. LN5 42 C1
St Marys St. LN5 42 C1
St Matthews Clo. LN5 42 A2
St Peters La. LN6 42 A6
St Peters Rd. LN6 42 A6
Sausthorpe St. LN5 42 C3
Saville St. LN5 42 B5
School La. LN5 43 E4
Scorer St. LN5 42 C3
Sewells Walk. LN5 42 B2
Shakespeare St. LN5 42 B3
Sibthorp St. LN5 42 C1
Sibthorp Gdns. LN5 43 E4
Sidney St. LN5 42 B3
Simons Grn. LN5 42 A6
Sincil Bank. LN5 42 C3
Sincil St. LN5 42 C1
Smiths St. LN5 42 B3
South Park. LN5 42 B4
South Park Av. LN5 42 B4
Spa Rd. LN2 43 E1
Spencer St. LN5 42 B3
Stamp End. LN2 42 D1
Stanley Pl. LN5 42 C2
Stanley St. LN5 42 B5
Sunningdale Dri. LN6 42 A3
Tanners La. LN5 42 B2
Tealby St. LN5 42 B3
Tentercroft St. LN5 42 C1
The Paddocks. LN5 43 E4
The Sidings. LN6 42 B1
Thesiger St. LN5 42 C2
Tritton Rd. LN6 42 A3
Trollope St. LN5 42 B6
Urban St. LN5 42 B6
Valentine Rd. LN6 42 A2
Vernon St. LN5 42 B2
Victoria St. LN5 42 C2
Waldo Rd. LN4 42 C6
Walnut Pl. LN5 42 C2
Washingborough Rd.
LN5 42 D3
Waterloo La. LN5 42 C1
Waterside Nth. LN2 42 C1
Waterside Sth. LN5 42 C1
Webb St. LN5 42 B3
Weir St. LN5 42 B4
Western Av. LN6 42 A4
Wigford Way. LN1 42 B1
Wyatt St. LN5 42 B4

## RUSKINGTON

All Saints Clo. NG34 49 B5
Arnhem Av. NG34 49 B4
Ash Tree Clo. NG34 49 C6
Beck Clo. NG34 49 A4
Beechtree Clo. NG34 49 C6
Bellview Rd. NG34 49 C5
Blackthorn Clo. NG34 49 C6
Bourne La. NG34 49 B4
Brauncewell Clo. NG34 49 A5
Brook Way. NG34 49 A4
Cedar Clo. NG34 49 B6
Chapel St. NG34 49 C5
Chestnut St. NG34 49 C5
Church St. NG34 49 C5
Church Vw. NG34 49 C5
Cliffe Av. NG34 49 A5
Cliffe Clo. NG34 49 A5
Cornwall Way. NG34 49 B4
Dorrington Clo. NG34 49 A5
East Clo. NG34 49 C5
Edinburgh Rd. NG34 49 B4
Elm Tree Clo. NG34 49 B5
Elm Tree Rd. NG34 49 B5
Fen Rd. NG34 49 C5
Field Clo. NG34 49 A4
Grange Clo. NG34 49 B4
Grange Rd. NG34 49 B5
Green La. NG34 49 A6
Haverholme Clo. NG34 49 D6
Hawthorn Clo. NG34 49 C5
High St Nth. NG34 49 C5
High St Sth. NG34 49 C5
Hillside Est. NG34 49 D5
Hollowbrook Clo. NG34 49 A4
Holme. NG34 49 C5
Horseshoe Clo. NG34 49 B4
Hurn Clo. NG34 49 B5
Jubilee St. NG34 49 A5
Leasingham La. NG34 49 A6
Lime Clo. NG34 49 B6
Lincoln Rd. NG34 49 B5
Manor Clo. NG34 49 B5
Manor St. NG34 49 C5
Meadowbrook. NG34 49 A4
Millview Rd. NG34 49 A5
Moor Pk. NG34 49 A5
Nene Clo. NG34 49 B4
Newton La. NG34 49 D5
Northfield Rd. NG34 49 C4
Park Lea. NG34 49 C4
Parkfield Rd. NG34 49 C4
Pinfold La. NG34 49 C4
Pinfold Way. NG34 49 C4
Poplar Clo. NG34 49 D5
Priory Clo. NG34 49 D5
Priory Rd. NG34 49 D5
Queensway. NG34 49 B4
Rectory Rd. NG34 49 A5
Roxholm Clo. NG34 49 A5
St Clements Rd. NG34 49 B5
Silver St. NG34 49 C5
Sleaford Rd. NG34 49 B4
Springfield Rd. NG34 49 B4
Station Rd. NG34 49 C5
Stray Grn. NG34 49 C5
Sycamore Rd. NG34 49 C6
Tennyson Rd. NG34 49 B5
The Firs. NG34 49 B5
The Orchards. NG34 49 D6
The Paddock. NG34 49 B5
The Sidings. NG34 49 B4
Tomlinson Way. NG34 49 C4
Walnut Clo. NG34 49 C5
Welland Clo. NG34 49 B4
West Beck. NG34 49 C4
West Gate. NG34 49 C4
West Rd. NG34 49 A5
Westcliffe Rd. NG34 49 A5
Whitehouse Rd. NG34 49 D4
Willow Clo. NG34 49 B6
Winchelsea Rd. NG34 49 B6
Witham Clo. NG34 49 B4

## SAXILBY

Almond Clo. LN1 52 C2
Ashfield Grange. LN1 52 A2
Blankney Clo. LN1 52 B2
Bridge Pl. LN1 52 C3
Bridge St. LN1 52 C3
Broadholme Rd. LN1 52 C3
Century La. LN1 52 B1
Church La. LN1 52 A1
Church Rd. LN1 52 B2
Danbury Av. LN1 52 B1
Eastcroft. LN1 52 B1
Elm Clo. LN1 52 C2

Forrington Pl. LN1 52 D2
Fossdyke Gdns. LN1 52 C2
Fosse Gro. LN1 52 C3
Gainsborough Rd. LN1 52 B3
High St. LN1 52 B2
Highfield Rd. LN1 52 B2
Hughes Ford Way. LN1 52 D3
Kenilworth Clo. LN1 52 B2
Lincoln Rd. LN1 52 C3
Lingfield Clo. LN1 52 B1
Macphail Cres. LN1 52 D2
Maiden Ct. LN1 52 D2
Manor Rd. LN1 52 B2
Meadow Rise. LN1 52 C1
Mays La. LN1 52 D2
Mill La. LN1 52 C1
Millfield Av. LN1 52 C2
Northcroft. LN1 52 B1
Northfield Rise. LN1 52 A2
Nursery Clo. LN1 52 C2
Oakfield. LN1 52 C2
Orchard La. LN1 52 B2
Otter Av. LN1 52 C2
Poachers Ct. LN1 52 C3
Queensway. LN1 52 C3
Rose Hill Clo. LN1 52 C2
St Andrews Dri. LN1 52 A2
St Botolphs Clo. LN1 52 C1
Salisbury Clo. LN1 52 B1
Skellingthorpe Rd. LN1 52 C3
Skirbeck Dri. LN1 52 B2
Sykes La. LN1 52 A1
South Par. LN1 52 B2
The Rowans. LN1 52 A2
The Sidings. LN1 52 B3
Thonock Dri. LN1 52 B2
Torksey Av. LN1 52 B2
Vasey Clo. LN1 52 D3
Warwick Clo. LN1 52 B1
Wentworth Clo. LN1 52 B2
West Bank. LN1 52 A3
Westcroft Dri. LN1 52 B1
Western Av. LN1 52 B2
William St. LN1 52 C3
Willow Clo. LN1 52 C2
Woodcroft Rd. LN1 52 A2
Woodhall Cres. LN1 52 B2

## SCUNTHORPE

Abercorn St. DN16 51 F5
Abey Gdns. DN15 51 E2
Agard Av. DN15 50 D4
Ajax Ct. DN15 51 E2
Alan Cres. DN15 51 E4
Albion Park. DN16 51 H6
Albourne Av. DN15 51 E5
Alexander Rd. DN16 51 G5
Alfreton Ct. DN15 50 A5
Allanby St. DN15 51 E4
Argyle Ct. DN15 51 F4
Ashbourne Ct. DN15 50 A4
Ashby Rd. DN16 51 E5
Ashdown Av. DN15 50 D3
Auckland Rd. DN15 50 D4
Avenswood La. DN15 50 B1
Avenue Cannes. DN15 50 B2
Avenue Clamart. DN15 50 B1
Avenue Fontenay. DN15 50 B1
Avenue Lourdes. DN15 50 B2
Avenue Rouen. DN15 50 B1
Avenue Vivian. DN15 50 C2
Avon Rd. DN16 51 G5
Axholme Rd. DN15 50 C5
Baildon Rd. DN15 50 C3
Bakewell Ct. DN15 50 A4
Banbury Rd. DN16 51 H5
Barnes Cres. DN15 50 D3
Baslow Rd. DN15 50 A5
Beech Av. DN15 50 A1
Belgrave Sq. DN15 51 F4
Bell La. DN15 51 E5
Belper Ct. DN15 50 A5
Berkeley St. DN15 51 E3
Bessemer Way. DN15 51 F2
Betony Clo. DN15 50 B1
Blackthorn Clo. DN15 50 A1
Bluebell Clo. DN15 51 G4
Bolsover Rd. DN15 50 A5
Boughton Av. DN15 50 D3
Brandon Rd. DN15 50 C5
Brant Rd. DN15 50 D4
Briar Way. DN15 50 B1
Bridport Wk. DN17 50 B6
Brigg Rd. DN15 51 G3
Brigg Rd. DN16 51 H5
Bruce St. DN15 51 E4
Brumby Wood La. DN17 50 B5
Buckingham Av. DN15 51 E1
Buckingham St Nth. DN15 51 E2
Buckingham St Sth. DN15 51 E3
Burke St. DN15 51 E3
Burke St Nth. DN15 51 E2
Burn Rd. DN15 50 A4
Burnham Rd. DN15 50 C5
Bushfield Rd. DN16 51 E6
Buxton Ct. DN15 50 A4
Carlton St. DN15 51 G4
Castella Dri. DN16 51 H4
Castleton Rd. DN15 50 A5
Cecile Cres. DN15 50 C3
Cedar Av. DN15 50 A1
Cemetery Rd. DN16 51 F5
Centenary Cotts. DN17 50 D5
Central Way. DN16 51 H5
Chaffinch Clo. DN15 50 C2
Chapel St. DN15 51 F3
Chatterton Cres. DN15 51 E2
Chesterfield Rd. DN15 50 A5
Church La. DN15 50 C5
Church Sq. DN15 51 G3
Clarke St. DN15 51 E4
Cliff Closes Rd. DN15 50 C4
Cliff Gdns. DN15 50 D4
Cliff St. DN16 51 G5
Cole St. DN15 51 F4
Colin Rd. DN16 51 H5
Collinson Av. DN15 50 B4
Coltsfoot Clo. DN15 50 B1
Comforts Av. DN15 51 E4
Commercial Rd. DN16 51 H4
Conway Sq. DN15 50 C4
Corby Rd. DN16 51 G5
Corporation Rd. DN15 51 F4
Cottage Beck Rd. DN16 51 E5
Cromwell Av. DN16 51 F5
Crosby Av. DN15 50 D1
Crosby Rd. DN15 51 F3
Cross St. DN15 51 F3
Dale St. DN15 51 E3
Dale St Nth. DN15 51 E2
Dartmouth Rd. DN17 50 B6
Davy Av. DN15 50 D3
Dawes La. DN15 51 G3
De Aston Sq. DN15 50 C4
Deacon Dri. DN15 50 A5
Denby Clo. DN15 50 C2
Derby Rd. DN15 50 A5
Detuyll St. DN15 51 E2
Detuyll St West. DN15 51 E2
Dewsbury Av. DN15 50 B3
Deyne Av. DN15 51 E4
Diana St. DN15 51 E2
Digby St. DN15 51 E3
Doncaster Rd. DN15 50 D4
Donnington Gdns. DN15 50 D4
Dowse Av. DN15 50 C3
Dronfield Ct. DN15 50 A4
Dunstall St. DN15 51 E4
Earl St. DN16 51 F5
Eastwood Ct. DN15 50 A5
Edgemere Ct. DN15 50 A4
Edwards Rd. DN15 50 D3
Elizabeth St. DN15 51 E3
Eryholme Cres. DN15 50 D4
Exeter Rd. DN15 50 D4
Fairfield Rd. DN15 50 B3
Fairmont Cres. DN16 51 F6
Farthing Av. DN15 50 C3
Fenton St. DN15 51 F4
Fernlea Clo. DN15 50 A1
Ferry Rd. DN15 50 B2
Ferry Rd West. DN15 50 A1
Fillingham Cres. DN15 50 A4
Fletcher Clo. DN15 50 B1
Flixborough Ftpth. DN15 51 E1
Fox St. DN15 51 E3
Foxhills Rd. DN15 50 C2
Frances St. DN15 51 F3
Frodingham Ftpth. DN16 51 F4
Frodingham Rd. DN15 51 E2
Fuchsia Croft. DN15 50 D5
George St. DN15 51 F3
Gervase St. DN15 51 E4
Giblin Cotts. DN15 50 D2
Gilliatt St. DN15 51 F3
Gladstone Dri. DN16 51 G6
Glanford Way. DN15 50 A4
Glebe Rd. DN15 51 F3
Glossop Rd. DN15 50 A4
Goldcrest Clo. DN15 50 C1
Grange Av. DN15 51 E2
Grassmoor Ct. DN15 50 A5
Grosvenor St Nth. DN15 51 E2
Grosvenor St Sth. DN15 51 E3
Gurnell St. DN15 51 F3
Haig Av. DN16 51 F6
Hallgarth Av. DN16 51 F5
Hargreaves Way. DN15 51 F1
Hartshead Av. DN15 50 B4
Hathersage Ct. DN15 50 A5
Haworth Clo. DN15 50 B3
Heanor Ct. DN15 50 A4
Hebden Rd. DN15 50 B3
Hempdyke Rd. DN15 50 C3
Henderson Av. DN15 50 D3
Henderson Cres. DN15 50 D3
Henry St. DN15 51 E4
Heron Clo. DN15 50 B1
Herriot Way. DN15 50 A3
High St. DN15 51 E4
High St East. DN15 51 G3
Highcliff Gdns. DN15 50 C4
Highfield Av. DN15 50 C4
Hilltop Av. DN15 50 C2
Hilton Av. DN15 50 A4
Holland Av. DN15 50 C3
Holmfirth Rd. DN15 50 B3
Home St. DN15 51 F3
Horbury Clo. DN15 50 C3
Hornsby Cres. DN15 50 D2
Hudson Av. DN15 50 D1
Ilkeston Ct. DN15 50 A4
**INDUSTRIAL & RETAIL:**
Berkeley Ind Est. DN15 50 A2
Kingsway Hi-Tech Business Pk. DN17 50 C6
Midland Ind Est. DN16 51 H6
Sawcliffe Ind Pk. DN15 51 F1
Ivanhoe Rd. DN16 51 H6
Jackson Rd. DN15 50 C4
Jellicoe Ct. DN16 51 G6
John St. DN15 51 F4
Jubilee Cotts. DN17 51 E5
Juniper Clo. DN51 50 A1
Kelsey Av. DN15 50 A4
Kenilworth Rd. DN16 51 G6
Kensington Rd. DN15 50 A4
Kettering Rd. DN16 51 G5
King Edward St. DN16 51 E6
King St. DN15 51 F3
Kingfisher Clo. DN15 50 B2
Kings Ct. DN15 51 F3
Kingsway Service Rd. DN15 50 B4
Kingsway. DN15 50 B4
Kingsway. DN17 50 C6
Laneham St. DN15 51 E4
Lavender Way. DN15 51 G4
Leamington Clo. DN16 51 G6
Leamington Ct. DN16 51 G6
Leonard Cres. DN15 50 D4
Lilac Av. DN16 51 G6
Lindsey St. DN16 51 G5
Lindum St. DN15 51 F4
Linnet Clo. DN15 50 B1
Lister Rd. DN15 50 B4
Little John St. DN15 51 F4
Lockwood Ct. DN15 50 C3
Lodge Rd. DN15 50 A5
Long Rd. DN15 50 C3
Luneburg Pl. DN15 50 B2
Luneburg Way. DN15 50 B1
Lydbrook Rd. DN16 51 E6
Lygon St. DN16 51 F5
Lynton Clo. DN15 50 B3
Main Approach Rd. DN16 51 H4
Maine Av. DN15 50 A1
Mallalieu Ct. DN15 50 D2
Manley St. DN15 51 F4
Mannaberg Way. DN15 51 E1
Mansfield Rd. DN15 50 A4
Maple Av. DN15 50 A2
Maple Tree Clo East. DN16 51 F6
Maple Tree Clo West. DN16 51 F6
Maple Tree Way. DN16 51 F6
Market Hill. DN15 51 F3
Marsden Dri. DN15 50 B4
Mary St. DN15 51 E4
Mary Sumner Way. DN15 50 C3
Matlock Ct. DN15 50 A5
Midland Rd. DN16 51 H5
Mill La. DN16 51 H4
Minster Rd. DN15 50 A5
Mirfield Rd. DN15 50 B3
Montrose St. DN16 51 F5
Moors Rd. DN15 50 A4
Mulgrave St. DN15 51 E2
Neath Rd. DN16 51 F6
Neville Rd. DN16 51 G5
Newborn Av. DN15 50 C3
Newcomen Way. DN15 51 G1
Newland Av. DN15 50 C5
Newland Dri. DN15 50 C4
Newland Wk. DN15 50 C4
Nightingale Clo. DN15 50 C1
Normanby Rd. DN15 51 E1
North Lincoln Rd. DN16 51 H5
North St. DN15 51 F3
Northampton Rd. DN16 51 G6
Northolme Cres. DN15 50 D4
Norwood Av. DN15 51 E5
Nostell Rd. DN16 51 H6
Old Crosby. DN15 51 E2
Old Ironside Rd. DN16 51 H4
Orchard Rise. DN15 50 D5
Oswald Rd. DN15 51 E4
Parkinson Av. DN15 51 E4
Pavilion Gdns. DN17 50 D5
Percival St. DN15 51 E3
Percy St. DN16 51 F5
Philips Cres. DN15 50 D4
Phoenix Parkway. DN15 50 B1
Pinchbeck Av. DN16 51 G5
Pippin Ct. DN15 50 B2
Plum Tree Way. DN16 51 F5
Plymouth Rd. DN17 50 B6
Poppy Clo. DN15 50 B1
Porter St. DN15 51 E3
Portman Rd. DN15 50 D1
Primrose Way. DN15 50 B1
Purbeck Rd. DN17 50 B6
Queen St. DN16 51 G5
Queensway. DN16 51 E6
Ravendale St Nth. DN15 51 F4
Ravendale St Sth. DN15 51 F4
Redbourn Clo. DN16 51 F6
Redbourn St. DN16 51 G5
Redbourn Way. DN16 51 F5
Reginald Rd. DN15 50 D1
Ripley Ct. DN15 50 A5
Robert St. DN15 51 F4
Robinson Clo. DN15 50 D3
Rose Wk. DN15 51 G4
Rothwell Rd. DN15 50 B3
Rowland Rd. DN16 51 E5
Russet Clo. DN15 50 B1
St James Ct. DN15 51 E4
St Marys Ct. DN15 50 B1
Sanderson Clo. DN15 51 F5
Sandhouse Cres. DN16 51 G6
Scotter Rd. DN15 50 B4
Scotter Rd. DN17 50 B5
Sedgewood Way. DN15 50 B1
Sheffield Pk Av. DN15 50 D2
Sheffield St. DN15 51 E3
Sheffield St East. DN15 51 E3
Sheffield St West. DN15 51 E3
Shelford St. DN15 51 F4
Shelroy Clo. DN15 50 B2
Sherburn Cres. DN15 50 C2
Sherwood Vale. DN15 50 C4
Skippingdale Rd. DN15 50 D1
Smith St. DN15 51 E3
Sorrel Way. DN15 50 A1
South Bank. DN15 51 F3
Speedwell Cres. DN15 50 A1
Spencer Av. DN15 50 D2
Stanley Rd. DN15 50 B3
Station Rd. DN15 51 E5
Stratford Dri. DN16 51 G5
Tanashi Dori. DN17 50 D6
Tansley Ct. DN15 50 A4
Teale St. DN15 51 E3
The Cliff. DN15 50 C4
The Close. DN16 51 F5
The Crofts. DN16 51 F5
The Fairways. DN15 50 A5
The Lilacs. DN16 51 G6
Theodore Gdns. DN15 50 D3
Theodore Rd. DN15 50 D3
Thompson St. DN15 51 F4
Tideswell Ct. DN15 50 A5
Tomlinson Av. DN15 50 D3
Trafford St. DN15 51 G3
Trent St. DN16 51 G5
Tulip Rd. DN15 51 G4
Vicarage Gdns. DN15 50 D5
Wares Way. DN15 50 A4
Warping Way. DN15 50 A4
Warren Rd. DN15 51 F2
Warwick Rd. DN16 51 G5
Webster Av. DN15 50 D4
Wells St. DN15 51 F3
West St. DN15 51 E3
Weymouth Cres. DN17 50 B6
Wilkie Clo. DN15 50 A4
William St. DN16 51 G5
Winn St. DN16 51 G5
Winterton Rd. DN15 51 F3
Woodale Clo. DN15 50 B1
Woodland Vw. DN15 50 B4
Woodstock Rd. DN16 51 H6
Wortley St. DN16 51 F5
Wybeck Rd. DN15 51 F1
Yarborough Ct. DN15 50 A5

## SKEGNESS

Abbey Clo. PE25 53 A2
Adrian Clo. PE25 53 A3
Albany Clo. PE25 53 A1
Albany Rd. PE25 53 A1
Albany Way. PE25 53 A1
Albert Av. PE25 53 C6
Albert Rd. PE25 53 B4
*Alexandra Ct, Alexandra Rd. PE25 53 B4
Alexandra Rd. PE25 53 B4
Algitha Rd. PE25 53 C3
Alma Av. PE25 53 A1
Alma Clo. PE25 53 A2
Alma Way. PE25 53 A1
Arcadia Cres. PE25 53 C4
Arcadia Rd. PE25 53 C4
Bader Way. PE25 53 A1
Barbara Rd. PE25 53 C5
Barnes Clo. PE25 53 A2
Barnes Rd. PE25 53 A2
Bayes Rd. PE25 53 B6
Beacon Way. PE25 53 A1
Beckett Clo. PE25 53 C5
Beech Rd. PE25 53 D5
Beresford Av. PE25 53 C4
Beresford Clo. PE25 53 C4
Beresford Cres. PE25 53 C4
Berry Way. PE25 53 B4
Beverley Gro. PE25 53 B4
Bracing. PE25 53 D4
Brancaster Dri. PE25 53 C1
Brian Av. PE25 53 B3
Briar Clo. PE25 53 C4
Briar Way. PE25 53 C5
Brisbane Clo. PE25 53 A2
Brunswick Dri. PE25 53 B2
Buckthorn Av. PE25 53 C6
Burdett Clo. PE25 53 A1
Burgh Old Rd. PE25 53 A1
Burgh Rd. PE25 53 A1
Burghley Rd. PE25 53 C6
Burlington Rd. PE25 53 A3
Butlin Clo. PE25 53 A2
Castleton Blvd. PE25 53 C2
Castleton Cres. PE25 53 C3
Cavendish Rd. PE25 53 C3
Cecil Av. PE25 53 C3
Charles Clo. PE25 53 A2
Cheshire Gro. PE25 53 A2
Church Rd. PE25 53 B2
Church Rd Nth. PE25 53 B2
Church Rd Sth. PE25 53 A3
Churchill Av. PE25 53 B1
Clarendon Rd. PE25 53 A3
Clifford Rd. PE25 53 B2
Clifton Gro. PE25 53 C5

## SKELLINGTHORPE

## SLEAFORD

Sycamore Dri. NG34 54 B2  
Tamer Ct. NG34 54 C3  
Tamson Way. NG34 54 C3  
Taunton Clo. NG34 54 B1  
Tennyson Av. NG34 54 A3  
The Blackthorns. NG34 54 B5  
The Drove. NG34 54 A3  
The Hoplands. NG34 54 D4  
The Innings. NG34 54 C5  
The Paddocks. NG34 54 C3  
The Reservation. NG34 55 E1  
Thomas St. NG34 54 B4  
Thrush Clo. NG34 54 A5  
Tower View. NG34 54 A6  
Town Rd. NG34 54 A6  
Trevitt Clo. NG34 54 A1  
Truro Clo. NG34 54 B1  
Vicarage Ct. NG34 54 C4  
Victoria Av. NG34 54 B5  
Walnutgarth. NG34 54 D5  
Watergate. NG34 54 B4  
Welby Clo. NG34 54 A3  
Wesley Clo. NG34 54 B5  
Wessex Clo. NG34 54 A6  
West Banks. NG34 54 B4  
Westgate. NG34 54 B4  
*Westgate Ct,  
  Westgate. NG34 54 B4  
*Wharfside Mews,  
  Carre St. NG34 54 C4  
Willow Ct. NG34 54 C5  
Winchester Way. NG34 54 B1  
Windsor Clo. NG34 54 A6  
Woodbridge Rd. NG34 54 D2  
Woodside Av. NG34 54 C1  
Woodside Clo. NG34 54 C1  
Woodside Vw. NG34 54 C1  
Wordsworth Ct. NG34 55 E4  
York Rd. NG34 54 B2  

## SPALDING

Aalsmeer Rise. PE11 56 A5  
*Abbey Pass,  
  Vine St. PE11 56 D4  
Abbey Pth. PE11 56 D3  
Abbots Way. PE11 56 A4  
Acacia Av. PE11 57 E2  
Acklam Av. PE11 57 F2  
Akita Clo. PE11 56 B6  
Albert St. PE11 56 A2  
Albion St. PE11 56 D3  
Aldwych Gdns. PE11 56 A6  
Alexandra Rd. PE11 56 D4  
Ambleside Dri. PE11 56 B5  
Amstel Clo. PE11 56 A5  
Amsterdam Gdns.  
  PE11 56 B5  
Angelica Dri. PE11 56 B1  
Annette Clo. PE11 56 B2  
Apeldoorn Gdns. PE11 56 B4  
Armstrong Rd. PE11 56 C5  
Arnhem Dri. PE11 56 C2  
Ash Ct. PE11 57 E2  
Atton Av. PE11 57 F2  
Avebury Gdns. PE11 57 F3  
Ayscough Av. PE11 56 D5  
Balmoral Av. PE11 56 D5  
Banbury Clo. PE11 56 D2  
Banks Av. PE11 57 E2  
Barge Clo. PE11 57 E2  
Barrier Bank. PE11 56 C6  
Bath La. PE11 56 D3  
Baxter Clo. PE11 57 F2  
Baxter Gdns. PE11 56 C1  
Beaufort Dri. PE11 56 C4  
Beckett Dri. PE11 56 C1  
Bedford Pl. PE11 56 D4  
Beech Av. PE11 57 E2  
Beechams Mews. PE11 56 B4  
Beechfield Gdns. PE11 56 D3  
Belcanto Ct. PE11 56 A2  
Belgrave Rd. PE11 56 B6  
Belisana Rd. PE11 56 A2  
Bellfield Clo. PE11 56 B4  
Belvedere Clo. PE11 56 B5  
Bentinck Clo. PE11 56 C1  
Birch Gro. PE11 57 E4  
Birkdale Clo. PE11 56 C6  
Bond St Ct. PE11 56 C3  
Bourne Rd. PE11 56 A4  
Bowditch Rd. PE11 56 D5  
Bramble Grange. PE11 56 B2  
Breda Ct. PE11 56 A5  

Brendon Wk. PE11 56 B1  
Bridge St. PE11 56 D3  
Britannia Gdns. PE11 56 C2  
Broad St. PE11 56 D3  
Broadway. PE11 56 A5  
Browns Gate. PE11 56 B3  
Buttercup Clo. PE11 56 A5  
*Butter Market,  
  Broad St. PE11 56 D3  
Camel Gate. PE12 57 F1  
Cameron Dri. PE11 57 E5  
Campbells Clo. PE11 56 B6  
Canterbury Clo. PE11 56 A3  
Carlton Clo. PE11 56 B6  
Carnoustie Cres. PE11 56 C6  
Carrington Clo. PE11 56 B4  
Carrington Rd. PE11 56 B3  
Castlefields. PE11 56 D2  
Cathedral Dri. PE11 56 C2  
Cavendish Way. PE11 56 C2  
Cedar Ct. PE11 56 D4  
Chaldean Way. PE11 56 C1  
Chambers Clo. PE11 56 B1  
*Chandlers Reach,  
  Church St. PE11 56 D4  
Chapel La. PE11 56 C3  
Charlette Way. PE11 56 A2  
Chaucers Way. PE11 56 A4  
Cherry Tree Gro. PE11 57 E2  
Chestnut Av. PE11 57 E2  
Childers North Dro.  
  PE12 57 F4  
Chiltern Dri. PE11 56 D1  
Church Gate. PE11 56 D4  
Church St. PE11 56 D4  
Churchill Dri. PE11 56 D5  
Clarence Gdns. PE11 57 E5  
Claudette Av. PE11 56 A2  
Claudette Way. PE11 56 B2  
Clay Lake La. PE11 57 E4  
Cleveland Clo. PE12 57 F3  
Cley Hall Dri. PE11 57 E3  
Cley Hall Gdns. PE11 57 E3  
Clover Way. PE11 56 B1  
Clumber Ct. PE11 56 C1  
Clydesdale Cres. PE11 56 A5  
Columbus Clo. PE11 56 C5  
Commercial Rd. PE11 57 E3  
Cook Dri. PE11 56 C5  
Cook Way. PE11 57 F1  
Corinne Gro. PE11 56 A4  
Coronation Clo. PE11 57 F2  
Cowbit Rd. PE11 56 C6  
Cradge Bank Rd. PE11 56 B6  
Cross Gate. PE12 57 G2  
Cross St. PE11 56 C4  
Crown Dri. PE11 57 F1  
Culpins Clo. PE11 57 F3  
Daniels Gate. PE11 56 C1  
Daniels Reach. PE11 56 C1  
Dawson Av. PE11 57 F1  
Delph Ct. PE11 56 B4  
Double St. PE11 56 D3  
Dowgate Clo. PE11 56 A4  
*Drapers Clo,  
  Gore La. PE11 56 D3  
Edinburgh Dri. PE11 56 D5  
Edinburgh Dri. PE11 57 E5  
Edward Rd. PE11 56 B3  
Ellen Cres. PE11 56 A4  
Elm La. PE12 57 G1  
Estella Way. PE11 56 A2  
Euston Av. PE11 56 B5  
Exeter Dri. PE11 57 E3  
Fairfield Clo. PE11 56 C1  
Fairview Way. PE11 56 C1  
Farrier Way. PE11 56 A5  
Farthingales. PE11 56 B1  
Fern Dri. PE11 56 C1  
First Av. PE11 56 A3  
Fleur Dri. PE11 56 D1  
Flinders Wk. PE11 56 C5  
Floriade Clo. PE11 56 B5  
*Foundry La,  
  The Crescent. PE11 56 D4  
Francis St. PE11 56 D3  
Fulney Av. PE11 57 F1  
Fulney Dro. PE12 57 G6  
Fulney La Nth. PE12 57 G1  
Fulney La Sth. PE12 57 G2  
Galway Clo. PE11 56 A2  
Gamlyn Clo. PE11 56 C5  
Gaunt Clo. PE11 57 F2  
Georgette Gdns. PE11 56 B2  
Glebe Clo. PE11 56 A3  
Glenn Av. PE11 56 C3  
Gore La. PE11 56 D3  

Gorse Way. PE11 56 C1  
Grange Dri. PE11 57 E3  
Green La. PE11 57 E4  
Greenrigg Gdns. PE11 56 D2  
Grevel Clo. PE11 56 B2  
Haarlem Ct. PE11 56 A5  
Hague Ct. PE11 56 B4  
Hall Pl. PE11 56 D3  
Halmer Gate. PE11 56 D4  
Halmer Paddock. PE11 57 E2  
Hannam Blvd. PE11 56 A4  
Harlequin Dri. PE11 56 A3  
Havelock St. PE11 56 D4  
Haverfield Rd. PE11 56 B4  
Hawthorn Bank. PE11 56 B4  
Heathfield Av. PE11 57 F5  
Helmsley Way. PE12 57 F3  
Henrietta St. PE11 56 C4  
Heren Pl. PE11 56 A5  
Hereward Rd. PE11 56 B3  
*Herring La,  
  Broad St. PE11 56 D4  
High St. PE11 56 D3  
Hoekman Ct. PE11 56 A5  
Hoekman Way. PE11 56 B5  
Holbeach Rd. PE11 57 E1  
Holborn Rd. PE11 56 B5  
*Hole in the Wall Passage,  
  Francis St. PE11 56 D3  
Holland Rd. PE11 56 D3  
Holyrood Wk. PE11 57 E5  
Horse Fayre Fields.  
  PE11 56 A5  
Horseshoe Rd. PE11 56 A5  
Hudson Rd. PE11 56 C5  
Hutton Clo. PE12 57 E5  
Ingleby Ct. PE11 57 F3  
Jacobs Ct. PE11 56 C1  
Johnson Av. PE11 56 D5  
Jubilee Clo. PE11 56 C3  
Julias Mead. PE11 56 B2  
Kellet Gate. PE12 57 G3  
Kensington Dri. PE11 56 B5  
Kings Rd. PE11 56 C3  
Kirby Ct. PE12 57 F3  
Knipe Av. PE11 56 C4  
Laburnum Gro. PE11 57 E2  
Ladywood Rd. PE11 56 D1  
Lancelot Way. PE11 56 B4  
Lansdowne Ct. PE11 57 F1  
Larch Clo. PE11 57 F4  
Lavender Dri. PE11 56 A5  
Law Ct. PE11 56 A2  
Leiden Flds. PE11 56 B5  
Lilburn Dri. PE11 56 C1  
Limburg Dri. PE11 56 A5  
Lime Ct. PE11 56 D4  
Lincoln Way. PE11 56 B2  
Linden Ct. PE11 57 E2  
Link Way. PE11 57 E3  
London Rd. PE11 56 B6  
Love La. PE11 56 D4  
Low Rd. PE12 57 F3  
Lowfields Av. PE12 57 F3  
Lucetta Gdns. PE11 56 C5  
Magellan Way. PE11 56 C5  
Mallard Rd. PE11 57 H4  
Mallory Clo. PE11 56 C5  
Malvern Av. PE11 57 E1  
Malvern Clo. PE11 57 E1  
Manor Clo. PE11 56 C6  
Mansell Clo. PE11 56 B4  
Maple Gro. PE11 57 E3  
Mariette Way. PE11 56 B2  
Marine Rd. PE11 57 E2  
Market Pl. PE11 56 D4  
Marlborough Av. PE11 56 D5  
Marsh Rails Rd. PE11 57 E5  
Matmore Clo. PE11 56 C6  
Matmore Gate. PE11 56 C5  
Mayfair Rd. PE11 56 B6  
Maytime Clo. PE11 56 A3  
Meadow Clo. PE11 57 E2  
Meadowgate La. PE11 56 A4  
Medcalfe Way. PE11 56 A3  
Medlock Cres. PE11 57 F2  
Mendip Clo. PE11 56 B1  
*Mercer Row,  
  Orchard St. PE11 56 D4  
Miles Bank. PE11 56 C1  
Monks House Clo. PE11 56 A4  
Monks House La. PE11 56 A4  
Monks Wk. PE11 56 A3  
Morus Clo. PE11 57 E5  
Muirfield Clo. PE11 56 C6  
Mulberry Way. PE11 57 E4  
Nene Ct. PE11 57 F2  

Neville Av. PE11 57 E3  
New Rd. PE11 56 D3  
Nicolette Way. PE11 56 B2  
Oak Ct. PE11 57 E4  
Oakley Dri. PE11 57 E2  
Orchard St. PE11 56 D4  
Osier Rd. PE11 57 E3  
Paddock Grn. PE11 56 D2  
Parkside Cres. PE11 56 C2  
Park Av. PE11 56 C2  
Park Clo. PE11 56 C1  
Park La. PE11 56 C2  
Park Rd. PE11 56 C3  
Patriot Clo. PE11 56 C2  
Paulette Ct. PE11 56 A2  
Pecks Drove East. PE12 57 F5  
Pecks Drove West.  
  PE12 57 F5  
Pennine Way. PE11 56 B1  
Pennygate. PE11 56 A4  
Pennyhill Clo. PE11 56 D1  
Percheron Dri. PE11 56 A5  
Pilgrims Way. PE11 56 A3  
Pilmore La. PE12 57 G2  
Pinchbeck Rd. PE11 56 C1  
Poplar Ct. PE11 56 A5  
Primrose Way. PE11 56 A5  
Priory Rd. PE11 56 C4  
Priory St. PE11 56 D4  
Quaker La. PE11 56 D4  
Queens Av. PE11 57 F1  
Queens Rd. PE11 57 F3  
Race Ground. PE11 56 A6  
Rainton Ct. PE12 57 F3  
Raleigh Ct. PE11 56 C5  
Rangell Gate. PE11 57 G3  
Red Lion St. PE11 56 D3  
Redthorne Clo. PE11 57 E2  
Regent St. PE11 56 C4  
Rembrandt Way. PE11 56 A5  
River Bank. PE11 56 C6  
*River Gate,  
  St Thomas's Rd.  
  PE11 56 C5  
Riverside. PE11 56 B2  
Roman Bank. PE11 57 F1  
Roman Brook. PE11 57 F1  
Roseleigh Way. PE11 56 C1  
Rowan Av. PE11 57 E2  
Rowan Way. PE11 57 F1  
Royce Rd. PE11 57 F1  
Rutland Clo. PE11 57 E3  
Saddlers Mead. PE11 56 A5  
St Andrews Rd. PE11 56 B6  
St Annes Clo. PE11 56 C1  
St Annes Way. PE11 56 D5  
St James Way. PE11 56 D5  
St Johns Dri. PE11 56 B4  
St Johns Rd. PE11 56 B4  
St Pauls Rd. PE11 57 E2  
St Thomas's Rd. PE11 56 C4  
Sandringham Wk.  
  PE11 56 D5  
Saxon Clo. PE12 57 E5  
Second Av. PE11 56 A3  
Severn Clo. PE11 57 F2  
Sezanne Wk. PE11 56 C2  
Shackleton Clo. PE11 56 C5  
Shearers Dri. PE11 56 A5  
Sheep Mkt. PE11 56 D3  
Sheila Cres. PE11 56 A4  
Sherwood Dri. PE11 56 D1  
Shire Av. PE11 56 A2  
Short St. PE11 56 D4  
Smithdale Clo. PE11 56 C1  
Snowdrop Pl. PE11 56 A3  
Sorrel Dri. PE11 56 A2  
South Par. PE11 56 D4  
Spalding Dro. PE12 57 E6  
Speyer Av. PE11 56 C4  
Spring Gdns. PE11 56 C4  
Spring St. PE11 56 C4  
Springfield Wk. PE11 56 C1  
Stables Ct. PE11 56 C4  
Station St. PE11 56 D4  
Stonegate. PE11 57 E4  
Sunningdale Av. PE11 56 C5  
Swan St. PE11 56 C3  
Tavistock Rd. PE11 56 D5  
Thames Rd. PE11 57 F2  
The Chantry. PE11 56 A3  
The Chestnut Av. PE12 56 D4  
The Crescent. PE11 56 D3  
The Green. PE11 56 D3  
The Grove. PE11 56 C5  
The Hayfields. PE11 56 B2  
The Meadows. PE11 56 C1  

The Parkway. PE11 56 A5  
The Vista. PE11 56 D4  
The Wende. PE11 56 A4  
The Wyke. PE11 56 A3  
Third Av. PE11 56 A3  
Thompson Clo. PE11 56 C4  
Thornton Rd. PE11 57 E5  
Tollgate. PE11 56 B3  
Tower La. PE11 56 D5  
Truro Clo. PE11 56 C3  
Two Plank La. PE11 56 B1  
Tulip Walk. PE11 56 C1  
Van Gogh Dri. PE11 56 A4  
Vernatts Grn. PE11 56 C1  
Victoria St. PE11 56 C4  
Victory Ct. PE11 56 C4  
Vikings Way. PE11 57 E5  
Vine St. PE11 56 D4  
Water La. PE11 56 C5  
*Waterside Ct,  
  Double St. PE11 56 D3  
Wedgewood Dri. PE11 56 A2  
Welbeck Dri. PE11 56 C2  
Welland Clo. PE11 56 C5  
*Welland Mews,  
  Double St. PE11 56 D3  
Welland Rd. PE11 56 C5  
Wensum Clo. PE11 57 F2  
Wentworth Clo. PE11 56 C6  
West Elloe Av. PE11 57 E1  
West Marsh Rd. PE11 57 E1  
West Par. PE11 56 B3  
Westbourne Gdns.  
  PE11 56 D4  
Westerly Way. PE11 56 A1  
Westlode St. PE11 56 D3  
Westminster Dri. PE11 56 B6  
Weston Hills Rd. PE12 57 H5  
Wheatmere Dro. PE12 57 H3  
Willesby Rd. PE11 56 D2  
Willow Wk. PE11 57 E3  
Windsor Dri. PE11 56 D5  
Winfrey Av. PE11 56 C3  
Wingate Mdws. PE11 56 B2  
Winsover Rd. PE11 56 B4  
Wintergold Av. PE11 56 C4  
Woodfield Clo. PE11 57 E5  
Woolram Wygate.  
  PE11 56 B2  
Wygate Pk. PE11 56 B2  
Wygate Rd. PE11 56 B3  

## SPILSBY

Alma Pl. PE23 61 D2  
Ancaster Av. PE23 61 C2  
Ancaster Wk. PE23 61 C2  
Ashby Mdws. PE23 61 D1  
Ashby Rd. PE23 61 C1  
Blind La. PE23 61 C1  
Boston Rd. PE23 61 C3  
Bowmans Ridge. PE23 61 B1  
Brickyard La. PE23 61 A2  
Church La. PE23 61 A1  
Church St. PE23 61 C2  
Erebus Clo. PE23 61 D3  
Eresby Av. PE23 61 C2  
Fitzjames Clo. PE23 61 D2  
Foxglove Clo. PE23 61 D2  
Grace Swan Clo. PE23 61 B2  
Halton Rd. PE23 61 D2  
High St. PE23 61 C2  
Hundleby Rd. PE23 61 B1  
INDUSTRIAL & RETAIL:  
  Vale Ind Est. PE23 61 C3  
Magellan Dri. PE23 61 D3  
Main Rd. PE23 61 A1  
Market St. PE23 61 C2  
Masonic La. PE23 61 B1  
Milners La. PE23 61 C2  
Newtown. PE23 61 D2  
North Beck La. PE23 61 A1  
Old Market Wk. PE23 61 C2  
Old School Mews.  
  PE23 61 D2  
Park Av. PE23 61 B1  
Partney Rd. PE23 61 C1  
Pooles La. PE23 61 C2  
Post Office La. PE23 61 C2  
Queen St. PE23 61 D2  
Raithby Hill. PE23 61 A1  
Resolute Clo. PE23 61 D3  
Reynard St. PE23 61 C2  
St James Wk. PE23 61 C2  
Shamfields Rd. PE23 61 D2

## STAMFORD

## SUTTON ON SEA

## WAINFLEET ALL SAINTS

## WASHINGBOROUGH

Butchers La. LN4   62 E4
Cambridge Dri. LN4   62 C2
Canterbury Dri. LN4   62 D3
Canwick Rd. LN4   62 B3
Carlton Mews. LN4   62 D3
Cavendish Mews. LN4   62 D2
Chapel La. LN4   62 D4
Chester Clo. LN4   62 D2
Church Hill. LN4   62 B1
Clarendon Ct. LN4   62 B2
Clarke Av. LN4   62 E4
Cliff La. LN2   62 B3
Cranbourne Mews.
  LN4   62 D2
Cromwell Clo. LN4   62 A2
Curtis Dri. LN4   62 D4
Curzon Mews. LN4   62 D2
Daniel Cres. LN4   62 D3
Daniel Gdns. LN4   62 D3
Deloraine Ct. LN4   62 B2
Drake Av. LN1   62 B2
Durham Cres. LN4   62 D2
Edward Barker Rd. LN4   62 E4
Enderby Clo. LN4   62 A2
Eton Rd. LN4   62 C2
Eve Gdns. LN4   62 D3
Exeter Clo. LN4   62 E2
Favell Rd. LN4   62 B2
Fen Rd,
  Heighington. LN4   62 F4
Fen Rd,
  Washingborough.
  LN4   62 C1
Fen View. LN4   62 F4
Ferry La. LN4   62 B1
Gail Gro. LN4   62 D3
Garratt Clo. LN4   62 D4
Gerrard Mews. LN4   62 D2
Gildesburgh Rd. LN4   62 B2

Gleneagles Gro. LN4   62 D2
Grange La. LN4   62 D4
Granson Way. LN4   62 A2
Grosvenor Mews. LN4   62 D2
Harrington Sq. LN4   62 E4
Harrow Clo. LN4   62 C2
Harvard Clo. LN4   62 D2
Hawthorn Clo. LN4   62 E3
Heighington Rd. LN4   62 A3
High Meadow. LN4   62 C2
High St,
  Heighington. LN4   62 D3
High St,
  Washingborough.
  LN4   62 B1
Hillcroft. LN4   62 A1
Hudsons La. LN4   62 E3
Jermyn Mews. LN4   62 D2
Julia Rd. LN4   62 D3
Keeble Dri. LN4   62 D2
Kenyon Clo. LN4   62 D4
Lee Av. LN4   62 D2
Leicester Clo. LN4   62 C2
Lincoln Rd. LN4   62 A1
Lindrick Clo. LN4   62 D4
Lintin Clo. LN4   62 D3
Lonsdale Ct. LN4   62 B2
Low Park La. LN3   62 F3
Lytham Clo. LN4   62 D2
Main Rd. LN4   62 B1
Malvern Av. LN4   62 D2
Manor Rd. LN4   62 B2
Marlborough Av. LN4   62 C2
Marlborough Ct. LN4   62 B2
Martin Clo. LN4   62 D4
Merrycock La. LN4   62 D4
Mill La. LN4   62 D3
Millers Clo. LN4   62 D3
Millstream Rd. LN4   62 D3

Mountbatten Ct. LN4   62 B2
Nelson Dri. LN4   62 B2
Newcot La. LN4   62 F4
Norwich Clo. LN4   62 E2
Oak Hill. LN4   62 B1
Old Stackyard. LN4   62 E3
Oundle Clo. LN4   62 C2
Oxford Clo. LN4   62 C3
Park Av. LN4   62 C2
Park Cres. LN4   62 C2
Park La,
  Heighington. LN4   62 E3
Park La,
  Washingborough. LN4   62 C2
Penfold La. LN4   62 C1
Pinder Clo. LN4   62 A2
Pitts Rd. LN4   62 C2
Potterhanworth Rd.
  LN4   62 E4
Queensbury Ct. LN4   62 B2
Raynor Clo. LN4   62 A2
Reading Clo. LN4   62 E2
Reption Clo. LN4   62 D2
Revesby Sq. LN4   62 E4
Rowan Ct. LN4   62 D3
Royal Oak La. LN4   62 C1
St Aubins Cres. LN4   62 E4
Sandra Cres. LN4   62 D3
School La. LN4   62 C1
Seely Ct. LN4   62 D3
Sheepwash La. LN4   62 C3
Sheppards Clo. LN4   62 D3
Station Rd. LN4   62 D4
Stevenson Clo. LN4   62 D4
Stoyles Way. LN4   62 D3
Sunningdale Gro. LN4   62 D2
Sutton Clo. LN4   62 A2
The Orchard. LN4   62 A1

Thornton Clo. LN4   62 A2
Thurlby Clo. LN4   62 A2
Trafalgar Ct. LN4   62 B1
Troon Clo. LN4   62 D2
Turnberry Clo. LN4   62 D3
Victoria Gro. LN4   62 D2
Washingborough Rd.
  LN4   62 C3
Wells Clo. LN4   62 E2
Wellsykes La. LN4   62 A4
Wentworth Clo. LN4   62 E2
Wheelwright La. LN4   62 E4
Willow Ct. LN4   62 C1
Winchester Dri. LN4   62 C2
Witham View. LN4   62 A1
Yale Clo. LN4   62 D2

## WOODHALL SPA

Albany Pl. LN10   63 A3
Albany Rd. LN10   63 A3
Alexandra Rd. LN10   63 A2
Alexandra Ter. LN10   63 A3
Alverston Av. LN10   63 B3
Arnhem Way. LN10   63 B3
Carnoustie Clo. LN10   63 A3
Clarence Rd. LN10   63 B2
Coronation Rd. LN10   63 A2
Cromwell Av. LN10   63 B3
Ebrington Clo. LN10   63 D2
Gorse Clo. LN10   63 C2
Green La. LN10   63 A1
Grove Ct. LN10   63 C3
Grove Dri. LN10   63 C3
Heather Clo. LN10   63 C2
Horncastle Rd. LN10   63 D1

Iddesleigh Rd. LN10   63 B2
King Edward Av. LN10   63 A2
King Edward Cres.
  LN10   63 A2
King Edward Rd. LN10   63 A2
King George Av. LN10   63 B2
Kings Wk. LN10   63 B2
Kirkby La. LN10   63 D2
Kirkstead Ct. LN10   63 C3
Long Av. LN10   63 B3
Maple Av. LN10   63 A1
Oak Clo. LN10   63 D2
Oaklands Av. LN10   63 A3
Park Clo. LN10   63 A2
St Leonards Av. LN10   63 C3
St Leonards Clo. LN10   63 A3
St Peters Dri. LN10   63 A3
Spa Ct. LN10   63 B2
Spa Rd. LN10   63 B2
Spa Trail. LN10   63 C1
Stanhope Av. LN10   63 B2
Station Rd. LN10   63 B2
Stixwould Rd. LN10   63 A1
Sylvan Av. LN10   63 C2
Tapleton Av. LN10   63 C2
Tattershall Rd. LN10   63 A3
The Broadway. LN10   63 B2
Tor-O-Moor Gdns.
  LN10   63 C2
Tor-O-Moor Rd. LN10   63 B3
The Close. LN10   63 A2
Troon Clo. LN10   63 A2
Turnberry Dri. LN10   63 B2
Victoria Av. LN10   63 B2
Wentworth Way. LN10   63 A3
Witham Rd. LN10   63 A3
Woodland Dri. LN10   63 C2